ROUTLEDGE LIBRARY EDITIONS: AFRICAN AMERICAN LITERATURE

Volume 1

THE FOREMOTHER FIGURE IN EARLY BLACK WOMEN'S LITERATURE

THE FOREMOTHER FIGURE IN EARLY BLACK WOMEN'S LITERATURE

Clothed in my Right Mind

JACQUELINE K. BRYANT

Routledge
Taylor & Francis Group

LONDON AND NEW YORK

First published in 1999 by Garland Publishing, Inc.

This edition first published in 2019
by Routledge
2 Park Square, Milton Park, Abingdon, Oxon OX14 4RN

and by Routledge
52 Vanderbilt Avenue, New York, NY 10017

Routledge is an imprint of the Taylor & Francis Group, an informa business

British Library Cataloguing in Publication Data
A catalogue record for this book is available from the British Library

ISBN: 978-1-138-38980-9 (Set)
ISBN: 978-0-429-42369-7 (Set) (ebk)
ISBN: 978-1-138-38958-8 (Volume 1) (hbk)
ISBN: 978-1-138-38973-1 (Volume 1) (pbk)
ISBN: 978-0-429-42374-1 (Volume 1) (ebk)

Publisher's Note
The publisher has gone to great lengths to ensure the quality of this reprint but points out that some imperfections in the original copies may be apparent.

Disclaimer
The publisher has made every effort to trace copyright holders and would welcome correspondence from those they have been unable to trace.

THE FOREMOTHER FIGURE IN EARLY BLACK WOMEN'S LITERATURE

CLOTHED IN MY RIGHT MIND

JACQUELINE K. BRYANT

GARLAND PUBLISHING, INC.
A MEMBER OF THE TAYLOR & FRANCIS GROUP
NEW YORK & LONDON / 1999

Library of Congress Cataloging-in-Publication Data

Bryant, Jacqueline K.
The foremother figure in early black women's literature :
clothed in my right mind / Jacqueline K. Bryant.
        p.   cm. — (Studies in African American history and
culture)
Based on the author's thesis (Ph. D., Kent State University)
Includes bibliographical references and index.
ISBN 0-8153-3380-3 (alk. paper)
1. American fiction—Afro-American authors—History and
criticism. 2. American fiction—Women authors—History and
criticism. 3. Domestic fiction, American—History and criticism.
4. Women and literature—United States—History. 5. Afro-
American families in literature. 6. Afro-American women in
literature. 7. Afro-Americans in literature. 8. Aged women in
literature. 9. Family in literature. I. Title. II. Series.
PS374.N4B73 1999
813.009'352042'08996073—dc21
                                                          99-13134

Printed on acid-free, 250-year-life paper
Manufactured in the United States of America

To My Mother, Mrs. Alberta B. Peterson
To My Father, Mr. James C. Peterson

Contents

Preface

Readers assume that the stereotypical mammy figure exists indiscriminately in nineteenth-century American literature; however, the older black woman portrayed in early black women's works differs substantially from the older black woman portrayed in early white women's works. The foremother figure, then, emerging in early black women's fiction revises the stereotypical mammy in early white women's fiction. In the context of the mulatta heroine the foremother produces minimal language that, through an Afrocentric rhetoric, distinguishes her from the stereotypical mammy and thus links her peripheral role and unusual behavior to cultural continuity and racial uplift.

Chapter 1 of this study provides background information on the mammy stereotype in southern white culture. Using close reading with a Womanist perspective, the following chapters examine speech situations in a series of works by white and black female authors. Chapter 2 shows how the mammy helps to define the ideal white female in response to a patriarchal ideology in six works by early white women writers such as Harriet Beecher Stowe, Carolyn Hentz, and Kate Chopin. Chapters 3 through 5 examine how the foremother figure helps to define the mulatta heroine in response to a racial uplift ideology. Chapter 3 differentiates the foremother from a strong mother figure in Harriet Jacobs's slave narrative, while Chapter 4 reveals the complexity and range of the foremother-mulatta relationship in three of Frances Harper's novels. In Chapter 5 two minor works by Pauline Hopkins illuminate the foremother-mulatta relationship in the motifs of passing and disguise. Similarly in Chapter 6 Jessie Redmon Fauset's four novels reveal the foremother-mulatta relationship in the context of passing. Chapter 7 concludes this study with an examination of three novels by later black women writers: Zora Neale Hurston, Ann Petry, and Gloria Naylor, and confirms the consistency of the positioning of the foremother and mulatta whether the relationship is liminal as in the early works of Hopkins or foregrounded as in the recent work of Naylor.

Acknowledgments

I wish to thank my dissertation committee members in the English Department at Kent State University, Kent, Ohio for their advice and support. A most emphatic thank-you to my advisor, Dr. Larry R. Andrews, who took the time to read numerous drafts of this study. I am indebted to him for his advice, responsiveness, and patience. A special thank-you to Dr. Martha J. Cutter, who also took the time to read drafts of this study and share her insight. A special thank-you also to Dr. Yoshinobu Hakutani, who has always been supportive and responsive over the years. I thank Dr. Denzel Benson and Dr. Raymond Craig for their willingness to serve as outside committee member and graduate representative, respectively.

I am indebted to the kindness and support of the Kent State University Honors College and English Department staff members, Ms. Diane Harris, Ms. Sally Yankovich and Ms. Dawn Lashua.

For those who expressed support, especially during the last eighteen months, I thank Dr. Molefi Kete Asante of Temple University, Drs. Howard A. Mims, Mittie Chandler, and Joan Baker, Sanza Clark, Earl Anderson, Adrienne Gosselin, Dolores Person Lairet, and Klaus Peter Hinze of Cleveland State University. A special thank-you to Dr. Wilhelmina Manns and Mrs. Beverly Gaffney. For their encouragement and assistance over the years I wish to thank Dr. Diedre Badejo, Dr. Melodie Baker, and Dr. Klaus Gommlich of Kent State University.

I offer my highest thanks and honor to God the Creator, the Ancestors, and my mother and father. I thank and honor my mother, Mrs. Alberta B. Peterson, and my father, Mr. James C. Peterson for their unyielding love, faith, and encouragement. A heartfelt thanks goes to my husband, Louis Bryant, for his ongoing support; to my dear daughter, Angela, for always having been a blessing to me because of her beautiful spirit and loving thoughtfulness; to my sister, Beverly Johnson, whose patience, understanding, and encouragement go unsurpassed; to each member of my extended family, I express sincere thanks.

Finally, a most emphatic thank you to The Reverend Dr. Otis Moss, Jr. for consistently imparting words of encouragement, cultural wisdom, and biblical instruction. A most sincere thank you for his biblical utterance that inspired the title of my study, "Clothed and in My Right Mind."

The Foremother Figure in Early Black Women's Literature

CHAPTER 1

Introduction

Stereotypical images of the black female exist in writings of white and black writers who published from slavery through the Harlem Renaissance and beyond. Black female images emerge as Aunt Jemima, Sapphire, Jezebel or wench, and mammy. Aunt Jemima is the cook who is dark in complexion, obese in size, and jovial in nature. Sapphire is headstrong and always emerges with the presence of the black male. She emasculates the black male with verbal put-downs. Her color is generally brown to dark brown. Jezebel is the bad, black girl who is generally the mulatta. She possesses white features and is portrayed with hypersexual behavioral characteristics. White men use her as the excuse for their sexual interactions (Jewell 1993, 46). The Jezebel/wench/mulatta is victimized when the white male blames her for promiscuous behavior consistent with the role which he himself has conceived, and when the white mistress perceives the casting of hypersexuality as a mockery of her own socially imposed purity (Gwin 1985b, 45). These images, which are believed to have evolved during slavery, portray African American women as the antithesis of the American conception of beauty, femininity, and womanhood (Jewell 1993, 36). Of these stereotypical images, the mammy, which emanated from the plantation, is considered to be the most persistent and enduring historically.

Because the plantation embodied the hierarchical structures of southern paternalism (Faust 1996, 32), it served as the primary site of social and political organization. Powerful white males occupied positions that controlled societal institutions and thus influenced societal ideas. White males, then, held the power to construct images. Many consider image construction humorous and a thing of the past, while others view its perpetuation as representative of larger problems in the society. Recognizing the significant impact that image construction must have had over time in this society has led to my probe into the literature of early black women writers in order to determine their role in combatting such action. In her essay entitled "Images of Black Women in Afro-American Literature: From Stereotype to Character" Barbara Christian (1985, 16) sees the construction of stereotypical images as inhumane action—essentially an act of racism reducing humans to a non-human level. She describes the early literary depiction of the mammy stereotype as a clay-like, silent figure and explains how, over time, this figure evolves into a character which represents a thinking and feeling being. To add to Christian's work, I will look at the effect of the language use of the older black woman in speech situations with the mulatta heroine or someone linked to the heroine in order to identify features of this language that propel the heroine toward action or change that ultimately affects individual, family, and/or community life.

SOCIO-HISTORICAL PERSPECTIVES ON BLACK FEMALE STEREOTYPES

In considering why the figure of the older black woman has moved from one form to another, it is helpful to view the socio-historical context which gave birth to stereotypes of black people and most importantly stereotypes of the black female. During the 1500s, when Europeans first established contact with blacks, they knew little about African cultures. Explorers and traders returned to their mother countries with fantastic stories that were based upon fear of the unknown and resulted in the creation of stereotypical figures. The majority of white men and women, never having had contact with Africans in their own habitat, relied on the observations of a few. These observations generally focussed on those physical characteristics and behaviors most unlike the Europeans, such as skin color, facial features, body type, and facets of the African lifestyle (Geist and Nelson 1992, 263-64). Before the eighteenth century, whites recognized blacks as different—as the other. They stressed the obvious contrasts in color, religion, and lifestyle, which included such negative descriptors as animality and sexual potency. Gradually, difference and stereotype became reasons to devalue and to create patterns of discrimination. During the mid-eighteenth century, black people, slavery, and subservience were synonymous if not in practice then certainly in the minds of members of the dominant culture (Foster 1993, 10).

The institution of slavery provided a legal basis for the establishment of specific hierarchical levels of domination and control. The patriarchal plantation fulfilled its role under this hierarchical system of governance, and one way in which its role is evident is in the construction of images. Powerful white men constructed the mammy image, and the patriarchal myth demanded it, but the question is why? According to Christian, nineteenth-century planters rationalized the patriarchal system by relying on scientific "proofs" that cast doubt on the humanness of the slave, and by perceiving themselves to be the patriarchs who existed in the Bible. The patriarchal system demanded obedience from wives, children, and slaves. The white female, above all the white wife, was a symbol of the white male's success; therefore, she could not work (1980, 8-10). Prenshaw discusses how writer George Fitzhugh in his 1854 book, *Sociology for the South*, describes southern white women in terms of their dependency. Any assertion of "independence" from white females, slaves, or children threatened the whole patriarchal system (1993, 77). Thus, if the image of the delicate white lady was to retain some semblance of truth, it would be necessary to create the image of another female based upon exaggerated reality and perceived needs and wants. The other female would be tough and could perform the duties of motherhood for the mistress and herself. As white women were pivotal to the preservation of white civilization through motherhood, black women were central to the continuation of the system of slavery and patriarchy through motherhood as an essential part of the American economy (Christian 1980, 7).

The southern planters' patriarchal myth is seemingly reinforced not only by the mammy's physical features and the tasks she performed, but by her natural cultural tendencies toward maternity. Black women held high regard for motherhood and maternal duties. This regard was maintained whether she was raped (infanticide and abortion were exceptional) or whether her state of motherhood was the result of consensual sexual relations. These views concerning motherhood held by most black women must have reinforced the southern planter's assumption that black women were innately suited for the role of mammies (Christian 1980, 11). In part, then, the existence of two different systems of values and beliefs provided a firm foundation for the maintenance of the stereotypical mammy. As Christian points out, however, a contradiction exists in a society which assigns the revered state of motherhood to a mammy, who is supposedly lower than animal (1980, 11).

Contradictions in the system and exaggerated contrasts between the ideal white female and the stereotypical mammy make one the correlate of the other. Christian argues that there could be no ideal white female in the imagination of a white patriarchal society without the black stereotypical mammy (1980, 12). Hazel Carby comes to a similar conclusion when she draws on Barbara Welter's attributes of "true [white] womanhood," which she describes as piety, purity, submissiveness, and domesticity. Carby explains that white women judged themselves by these parameters just as the white male and society judged them (1987, 23). The image of the ideal white lady was essential for the patriarchal societal dream, but it could not have been imagined, created, or perpetuated without the correlate of the stereotypical mammy, who was not really defined as woman at all, according to Carby. The image of the lady and its correlate, the mammy, were essential components of the South's public dream and thus its literature (Christian 1980, 11). The work of white woman writer Caroline Lee Hentz, for example, contains numerous instances that embody stark contrasts between the white female and the black woman regardless of whether the former holds the role of mistress and the latter of mammy. In Hentz's *The Planter's Northern Bride* (1854), the hero, Moreland, enters the humble abode of a black woman, Nancy. Also present is a white female, Eula, to whom Moreland is very attracted. The narrator verbalizes Moreland's thoughts and forces the reader to see through Moreland's eyes that Nancy's cottage is dark and low. Nancy reflects death because she is variously described as poor, pale, and emaciated. Eula reflects life because she is variously described as lively, youthful, and healthy: "Her skin is soft and like the paleness of moonlight" (1:46). The contrasts of light and dark, good and sinister communicated through the conduit of Moreland's thoughts exemplify early nineteenth-century southern ideology. Without conscious malice or premeditated motive such contrasts were the social norm and thus flourished in the literature.

Despite the over-simplicity of such stark contrasts in literature, however, the relationship of mammy to white mistress was complex. The Civil War illuminated that the gulf between them was not as great as it seemed. According to Drew Gilpin Faust some slave mistresses in isolated areas of the South found that their closest adult connections were with female slaves (1996, 61). With the departure of so many men to battle, the Confederate home front became a world of white women and slaves (31), and "faithful servant" stories served to calm the fears of the white female (61). White females of the southern elite came face to face not only with fear, but also with the realization that their notion of womanhood had presumed the existence of slaves to perform menial labor and white males to provide protection and support. "Lady," then, meant whiteness and privilege; elite status had been founded on the oppression of slaves, and the notions of genteel womanhood had been intertwined with class and race (7).

Still another dimension of the complex relationship between the white female and the mammy is that the latter was generally second to the mistress in authority. Michelle Wallace explains that the black woman slave achieved status in her role as mammy because she often controlled the household, its white members as well as the black. Even though she sometimes guarded the master's wealth and position with loyalty and vigor, the mammy often served a useful function for the slave community when she interceded on behalf of a slave and aborted cruel punishment (1991, 21). The multiplicity of her roles permitted her to serve in the big house and maintain her link with her own community members in the field.

CULTURAL IMAGERY AND THE MAMMY STEREOTYPE

After considering the origin and maintenance of the stereotype of the black female, I am compelled to ask the following question: Why did the perpetuation of black female stereotypical images continue after emancipation? One of the objectives of cultural imagery is not only to legitimize and perpetuate stereotypes but also to encourage individuals to embrace certain values and beliefs. Through systematic exposure to cultural images, individuals are expected either to conform to, emulate, and internalize the characteristics, values, beliefs, and behaviors of these images, or to reject them and accept those images that are diametrically opposite (Jewell 1993, 69). In each case, cultural images were constructed by those in power based on exaggerated reality and embellished truths, and perpetuated by members of the society. Each image was designed to justify the treatment that black women received during slavery. Cultural images that assign virtue and an assumed level of intellectual ability to the occupation, behavior, and appearance serve to elevate the status of one group above another in a given society (Jewell 1993, 58).

Again, these cultural images were constructed by powerful white males, purveyed by the media that they influenced, and perpetuated by members of the society in order to maintain a system of domination. The construction of cultural images was yet another attempt to control blacks in general. As conveyed in popular wisdom, he who controls the image, controls the mind. To produce images is to define, and to define is another level of control. K. Sue Jewell says that it is reasonable to presume that the cultural images of black women were important economically after emancipation in order to keep black women and others outside the economic mainstream (1993, 56). Those who controlled the images then not only controlled the minds but controlled the wealth. Jewell's *From Mammy to Miss America and Beyond: Cultural Images and the Shaping of U.S. Social Policy* (1993) provides in-depth discussion of each stereotypical image of the black female from antebellum literature to the mass media today. She discusses the purposes for the construction and maintenance of specific stereotypical images which have changed over time but still remain in some form today. My investigation differs from Jewell's in that she looks at stereotypes in relation to the larger society, while I look at the figure of the older black woman historically stereotyped as the mammy in the smaller society of the black community. To determine the purpose of the older black woman in early black women's literature is central. In her scope of the larger society, Jewell concludes that one purpose for maintaining stereotypical images of black women is to elevate the status of other groups, which again points to the underlying desire for not only economic control, but hegemony, which spans every aspect of the domination of one group over another.

The period of Reconstruction was a significant phase in American history when hegemonic notions heightened aggression for economic and political control. Black males were granted the right to vote in 1870; therefore, those in the political arena saw the black man not only as a political opponent, but as a former slave—powerless and noncompetitive. Regardless of how they were perceived, blacks sought political representation, education, land and small business ownership, and employment. Blacks were moving into new areas of society. To maintain domination and control whites required not only aggression, but regression as a form of subjugation. In addition to establishing Jim Crow laws and using lynch violence, whites went to great lengths to "prove" that blacks were physically and intellectually inferior to whites. Cultural imagery, then, was merely a form of continuing social control and explains why stereotypical images were perpetuated following emancipation and why the features of, especially, the stereotypical mammy are familiar to members of American society even today.

Jewell describes the stereotypical mammy's physical features as obesity, dark complexion, extremely large breasts, extremely large buttocks, and shining white teeth; she is depicted wearing a head scarf, and her extreme obesity is seen as matronly and humorous (1993, 39). The portrayal of the mammy as overweight is not accidental, because this physical feature moves the mammy outside the sphere of sexual desirability and into the realm of maternal nurturance (1993, 40). In concert with her physical features, the mammy's personality is portrayed as kind, loyal, religious, and superstitious; she is a mother who is actually viewed as sexless because she is portrayed as ugly. As a mother, she exhibits a preference for her master's children to her own, and she acknowledges, instinctively, the superiority of the higher race (Christian 1980, 11). The mammy, then, not only contributes to the maintenance of the stereotype, but, according to Christian's observations, confirms the myths, the imagined hierarchical levels, and the general expectations of those who benefitted from the patriarchal system. In *Black Women Novelists: The Development of a Tradition, 1892-1976* (1980), Christian traces the development of stereotypical images imposed on black women and assesses how these images affected the works of black women from 1892 to 1976. My study looks back to representative works of both black and white women who published prior to 1892, and it includes Frances Harper's older novels rediscovered since Christian's work.

LITERARY IMAGES OF THE MAMMY

The image of the mammy in early white women's literature challenged critics who argued that slavery was harsh and demeaning. Jewell describes the behavioral characteristics of the mammy in this literature and other media as follows: a) she is submissive to her slave owner during slavery and to her employer following slavery; b) she is aggressive in her relations with other African Americans, especially males; c) she appears satisfied and content in her station in life (1993, 38).

With her ultimate obedience a given, the mammy figure could still be defined and portrayed as independent, aggressive, and decisive. Those in power perceive these qualities to be masculine and therefore negative because such features are exaggerated when associated with images that represent black women (Jewell 1993, 46). An example of this negative association occurs in Harriet Beecher Stowe's *Uncle Tom's Cabin* when Miss Ophelia observes how Dinah supervises the kitchen detail. Meal preparation takes place on the kitchen floor as Dinah rules over her kitchen help. The text describes Dinah's methods as "peculiarly meandering and circuitous" (1966, 225) because in her own unique way she acts decisively, and because she is controlling in her attempts to discourage Miss Ophelia from entering the kitchen. Dinah is depicted as eccentric, secretive, and in some ways threatening. Bent on keeping her position in the power hierarchy, she therefore confirms the hierarchy and her own ultimate obedience. In some cases, however, the negative, aggressive element is so pronounced that it counters the image of submissive and loyal contentment. Variations on the stereotype portray the mammy as cunning, prone to poison her master, discontent with her lot, fierce in protecting her children, and conniving against the system of bondage. (Christian 1985, 5)

Whether the focus is her physical, behavioral, or emotional characteristics, the mammy figure resides in the consciousness of the nation and thus in its works. For example, although most critics ignore Mammy Jane in the critique of Charles W. Chesnutt's *The Marrow of Tradition*, dismissing her as functional in her roles of nursemaid, cook, etc., she reveals significant attitudes. Because Chesnutt creates such a character, Trudier Harris views Mammy Jane critically and determines that her behavior, which is indicative of enslavement, speaks volumes about her portrayal in a literary work set during the period of Reconstruction. Mammy Jane's subservience reflects the attitudes of whites who longed for the days of slavery as well as the attitude of blacks who longed for nothing more than to continue in an attitude of subservience (1982, 39). Langston Hughes inscribes a similar attitude of subservience in the figure of an older black woman in his novel *Not Without Laughter* (1930). Calvin Hernton discusses Langston Hughes's characterization of his grandmother in *The Sexual Mountain and Black Women Writers: Adventures in Sex, Literature and Real Life*. Hughes depicts his grandmother as a laundress for white folks. He also depicts her as uneducated, religious, and emphatically African American in appearance, speech, and manner. Hughes admits that he exaggerated this fictional character to make her appear more "negro." In actuality, his grandmother did not provide laundry service for white folks, nor did she attend church, and she did possess an education (1987, 91). The compulsion to perpetuate stereotypical images is understandable when one considers the mechanisms that were in place to maintain them, such as a patriarchal ideology that limited what could be published and that resulted in audience expectations. Thus as Harris suggests, writers such as Chesnutt worked within the system and used accommodation subversively in his portrayal of the mammy in order to underscore the vestiges of slavery while Hughes, at times, chose to portray his mammy figure in order to fulfill audience expectations.

THE EARLY BLACK WOMAN WRITER—CONTEXT AND TEXT

During the late nineteenth century, social changes made a significant impact on the relationship between white and black female writers. It was an era that saw the end of slavery and the beginning of greater voice for women's issues. The color line divided white and black women writers as it divided the nation. Their interests developed along separate paths (Foster 1993, 82). Both black and white female writers, however, were concerned with revising, deconstructing, and reconstructing images of women inherited from male literature, but the struggle for black women writers was against white male inherited images *and* the perpetuation of those clay-like images by white women writers (Foster 1993, 82-83).

Christian speaks of black female characters as thinking and feeling people despite the clay stereotypes permanently cast in white literature (1985, 14). In Phillipa Kafka's Introduction to *The Great White Way*, she comments that black women writers are both African American and European American culturally. This makes their response to European American, male-dominated success mythologies more complex than had they been simply European American women writers like Kate Chopin (1993, 14). Most black writers who have created stereotypical maids and mammies have had specific goals in mind for their creations. The goals were frequently dictated by the time periods in which authors wrote, as well as by their degree of commitment to changing the social advancement of black people. Some may have even used character design to spark political consciousness and black awareness among blacks (Harris 1982, xiv). A writer often used a very different and unlikely character in order to instruct her audience. Figuratively, it is the character hovering on the periphery of society that has the ability to see and thus to express contrasting ideologies, question assumptions, and topple fundamental beliefs. The periphery is a different location, and thus a different viewpoint. It varies from the norm, the expected, and quite naturally it results in a different and often inexplicable perspective.

Foster disagrees with the assertion that early black writers adopted forms and techniques of western literature and addressed their remarks to a white audience. Such an assumption devalues the relationship between black writers and black readers, and it disregards the vitality and versatility of the black culture. Foster believes instead that the early black woman writer appropriated the English literary tradition to reveal, to interpret, to challenge, and to change perceptions of herself and the world in which she found herself (1993, 15-16).

The early black woman writer knew in part that her act of writing tested social attitudes because she was all too aware of how white men scrutinized Phyllis Wheatley's work to determine the legitimacy of her authorship during the late eighteenth century. The black woman writer could not proclaim the importance of her word as the privileged white male such as Thomas Jefferson proclaimed the importance of his. She knew her gender and race infused her words with connotations which were complex and difficult to control (Foster 1993, 17). The black woman writer was painfully aware that when nineteenth-century blacks wrote in a manner that did not correspond to those deeply held opinions of the times, their very authorship was put into question. Such a restriction could have obliterated their very existence, and would have certainly affected the way they wrote about blacks (Christian 1990, 332).

If the act of writing tested societal attitudes, then the early black woman writer wrote to reform as well as transform her audience, since often her focus was spiritual and moral reformation which resulted in home and community transformation. According to Jewell, transformation requires that one eradicate stereotypes, dispel myths, and supplant ideologies that serve as the bases for systems of domination (3).

INTRODUCTION OF THE FOREMOTHER FIGURE

In an effort to understand these early writers' use of a stereotype it is important to look beyond the surface of the generalized stereotype and to look closely and critically at the image of the older black woman in early black women's literature to determine the purpose of her presence. I propose that the image of the older black woman does not fit the stereotypical mammy image perpetuated by white women writers in their antebellum literature or by the post-war plantation school. I believe that a change in the name and the definition will promote recognition of the differences that exist between the older black female portrayed in early white women's writings and the older black female portrayed in early black women's writings. I will thus rename and redefine the character portrayed by black women writers as the "foremother figure." The foremother figure is actually a character who has presence without prominence and displays force without the benefit of a place in the foreground. The term "foremother" is suggested by Alice Walker (1983b) in her essay, "In Search of Our Mothers' Gardens," where she explains that this black woman is the one who prepared, molded, and created despite constraints such as physical and mental abuse, inadequate space and materials, and the intrusion of her own children and household responsibilities. By whatever means, these grandmothers, mothers, and older black women in general passed on creative genius in the forms of storytelling, language style, color coordination, and design inside and outside the home. One can add to this image of artistry in the foremother figures in Schultz's observations that they suffer, endure, and maintain a strong faith in God. They do not engage in active resistance, but they are never passive but always building and creating (1977, 341). Mary Hughes Brookhart's quotation from Paule Marshall's *Praisesong for the Widow* captures yet another dimension of the endowed ancestor or foremother in the following: "'those pure-born Africans was peoples . . . [who] could see in more ways than one . . . the kind can tell you 'bout things happened long before they was born and things to come along after they was dead'" (1993, 129). Even though the supernatural may be associated with these women, they are also great in the most familiar ways. Authors speak of how these women gather daughters into their arms—daughters in need of healing. These sometimes non-biological mothers nurture fledgling daughters in order to rid them of their self-destructive behavior brought on by oppression (Brookhart 1993, 135).

The foremother is further a moral and cultural reservoir who is unaware of the intensity of her own spirituality and the knowledge of her own sainthood. She is a complex figure, a vessel which preserves and passes on creative genius as well as one who preserves and conveys wisdom. The foremother is a visionary who knows what is to be. She possesses a hope so intense that it directs circumstances. She nurtures, advises, teaches, protects, and directs those who have the privilege of being in her presence. The foremother loves with tenderness and with toughness. She is blessed by the ancestors and abides by their counsel; thus she possesses the capability to discern truth. I propose that this powerful foremother figure can be defined through the narrative, the direct and indirect language associated with the character, and the direct and indirect language of the heroine and other major and minor characters.

Not all texts portray this ideal construction of the foremother figure. The foremother figure is less than ideal insofar as she emerges in the likeness of the stereotypical mammy, e.g., Hopkins's Aunt Henny. Some foremothers are also clearly flawed in their influence in the life of the mulatta heroine, e.g., Fauset's Hetty.

The construction of the foremother in early black women's works helps, then, to define the mulatta heroine in that the foremother's language functions as a cultural source which influences the heroine's view of the world, her decisions, and/or her actions. The language of the foremother is grounded in the substance of the culture and the knowledge of her experience. In speech situations that include the mulatta or a character linked to the mulatta, the language of the foremother emerges as a feature of character that effects change. The language of the foremother effects change whether she is ideal or flawed. She influences others, that is, whether she adheres to the general qualities of the foremother outlined above or whether she exhibits variability in these character traits. Her language, although limited, simple, and often repetitive, is powerful and connects clearly and meaningfully to the life of the mulatta heroine. Whether the mulatta heroine is a direct or an indirect recipient of her words, the authoritative older black woman influences the mulatta heroine with her wisdom. Even if the latter does not always immediately recognize or deliberately ignores this and other positive qualities in the discursive matrix as a voice of wisdom, the foremother still exists, persists and frequently the resistant heroine eventually yields to her positive influence (Hopkins's Hagar) or becomes reconciled to her flaws (Hurston's Janie). For example Aunt Henny emerges as the stereotypical mammy in *Hagar's Daughter* when she is more protective of her mistress, Hagar, than she is of her own daughter, Marthy. Aunt Henny tells Marthy, "'I don' no 'bout tellin' a disrespons'ble gal like you fambly secrets . . . '" (63). Mrs. Harcourt in Harper's *Trial and Triumph* initially uses the power of her words to silence Annette's insightful description of a neighbor's disposition when she says: "'You give me more worry than all my six children put together; but there is always one scabby sheep in the flock and you will be that one'" (184). The foremother figure is as meaningful in the preceding portrayals as she is when portrayed as a model—a model who generates language activity that results in social action on the part of the mulatta heroine, as in Harper's *Iola Leroy*. Aunt Linda calls for a leader who will "'larn dese people how to bring up dere chillen, to keep our gals straight, an' our boys from runnin' in de saloons an' gamblin' dens'" (160-61). Ultimately Iola emerges as a moral community leader when she tells Aunt Linda, "'I am going to teach in the Sunday-school, help in the church, [and] hold mothers' meetings to help these boys and girls to grow up to be good men and women'" (276). The older black woman's language activity informs the younger mulatta heroine's practical activity, which then results in social action that makes a difference in the community.

Age is a significant factor in the portrait of the foremother in early black women's literature. Alice Walker refers to Jean Toomer's comments on the authoritative older female and concludes that she is more than a mere woman—she is a saint. The foremother is sanctified, that is, she is set aside for some spiritual use. The foremother figure exists in Walker's observation about Phyllis Wheatley that it is not so much that she sang, but that she kept the notion of the song alive (Walker 1983b, 237). In other words it is not radical pro-action or even reaction, but liminal or barely perceptible aspects of the culture that are cherished and maintained in the embodiment of the foremother figure. She is the life-force that nurtures her own culture as she repels the influences of the dominant culture that are all too often realized in thought, word, and behavior. The foremother's world view acts as a protective shield that aids in narrowing the focus to make one see more clearly. The role of the mammy, then, is carefully and continually moved from the status of stereotype to that of a living human being who is aware of her own desires and needs but places them second to those of the community. Thelma Shinn comments on modern writer Octavia Butler's recreation of the older black woman in her works when she refers to her as the wise old witch within the archetype of the older black woman who is willing to share her survival skills out of compassion and a sense of responsibility with those who are still willing to learn (1985, 214). Such a description connotes the relationship that the older black woman maintains with the community. The needs of the community remain a priority.

Because of the black woman's existence, her experience of and expression of her reality is often culturally distinct; therefore, her perception when verbalized is a strong statement about her condition (Christian 1985, 14). The generative power of her words is embedded in the texts of early black women writers, and this study seeks to determine how early black women writers constructed the language of the foremother in order to weaken the hierarchical structures that strained to keep that clay-like, non-thinking, non-feeling image of the loyal, submissive stereotype in place.

To debunk the image of the stereotypical mammy is to debunk the western ideology of a white male power structure and its system of hierarchy. Trudier Harris argues that some early black male and black female writers chose to portray black women in literature who held on to a sense of self against forces that would stereotype them, force them to conform, or dehumanize them. Of the women writers' heroines she cites Nella Larsen's Helga Crane (1928) and Zora Neale Hurston's Janie Crawford (1937) (Harris 1982, xiii). It is likely that later black women writers recognized the often veiled efforts of early black women writers to construct authentic characterization within the constraints of publication. According to Joanne Gabbin, contemporary black women writers have begun to explore the roots of their cultural tradition and are cleansing, healing, and empowering the images of themselves (Gabbin 1990, 247). Gabbin draws on the works of contemporary writers such as Toni Cade Bambara, Zora Neale Hurston, Margaret Walker, Toni Morrison, and Paule Marshall, who "possess" their images and define themselves as they explore the roots of the cultural condition by confronting the past.

In this proposed re-vision of the image of the black woman, the mulatta stereotype is also relevant. The mulatta character occurs occasionally in white women's writings but more often in black women's abolitionist writings. Southern writers during the antebellum period focussed on the black woman as the contented mammy rather than as the mulatta, since the mulatta represented miscegenation, which whites attempted to ignore (Christian 1980, 16). The mulatta, however, appears alongside the stereotypical mammy image in black women's writings, especially during Reconstruction, post-Reconstruction, and the Harlem Renaissance. Specifically, the image of the older black woman, who is present but not prominent in the literature, plays a significant role in her relationship with the mulatta, even in her seemingly muted state.

Why did the mulatta become a staple in early black literature? Alice Walker compares the literary portrayal of the mulatta and white-complexioned female to the black-complexioned female in her essay entitled, "If the Past Looks Like the Present then What Does the Future Look Like?" (1983a). She focusses on the absence of the truly black woman in mainstream black middle-class society. She turns to the literature of early black women writers for answers pertaining to those characters who are seemingly portrayed as black people but who cherish the white blood that stripped their black foremothers of their womanhood. Studying three nineteenth-century novels written by black women: Frances Harper's *Iola Leroy or Shadows Uplifted* (1892), Pauline Hopkins's *Contending Forces: A Romance Illustrative of Negro Life North and South* (1900), and Emma Dunham Kelley's *Megda* (1891), Walker focusses on the dialogue of particular characters and describes how they rave over the beauty of the mulatta heroine. Walker questions why black women writers depicted their heroines as white and non-working class. She also speaks strongly against the early black male novelist, William Wells Brown, and others who portrayed their heroines as indistinguishable from whites (295). Walker concludes that these imagined quadroon women were not real and had more to do with the way white men chose to perceive black women than the way black men perceived them or black women perceived themselves (298). Walker further reasons that black women writers used white-skinned heroines in nineteenth-century literature because most of their readers were white; whites could associate human feeling with whiteness or near whiteness. Emma Dunham Kelley's *Megda* provides an excellent example in Megda's best friend, depicted in the death scene: "Ethel was lying on the bed, her face as white as the pillow on which it rested, her fair hair surrounding it like a golden cloud. She smiled when she saw Meg and held out a white hand" (337). The emphasis on whiteness is repeated throughout the novel when associated with young females. Black men can be depicted as dark because darkness connotes masculinity, but whiteness connotes femininity in the European American mind. To portray the dark-skinned black woman would have reinforced the stereotyped perception of the masculine black female (Walker 1983a, 301).

Like Walker, Christian believes that black women writers used the mulatta to secure white women readers' sympathy with black women. The emphasis on the plight of the mulatta then developed into a tradition in black women's writings. Christian suggests that white readers saw the result of their domination of another people in the portrayal of the mulatta. She concludes that the guilty and powerful enjoy looking obliquely at their own guilt. The mulatta speaks clearly to the workings of domination and control, but on the other hand, the mulatta was an effective means to show that no differences existed between a black and white woman until someone discovered or decided that one drop of negro blood made a difference (Christian 1985, 3). Although the white audience dealt with the delicate issues surrounding the mulatta, the mammy was the familiar mainstay image that they expected in the literature because she was subsumed in the ideology of a patriarchal society.

To look at the foremother figure in the context of the mulatta heroine, the mammy again becomes the foil or the correlate. One can make similar contrasts between the foremother and the mulatta as others have done between the stereotypical mammy and the white female. The mulatta heroine is described as beautiful, with long flowing hair and light-colored eyes; the mulatta heroine has voice, choice, and some level of authority. We hear the voice of the mulatta abundantly in dialogue because she is usually the protagonist. She has choice in that she generally has the option to pass as white. With that choice she thus assumes some level of authority. An emotional tension surrounds the mulatta, however, because she is the beautiful female who represents the illicit crossing between the cultures. The underlying fear that others will discover that she is a member of the black race is always present. The discovery generally emerges through family relations, slave traders, or the birth of the mulatta's child. The mulatta's color is a constant and disturbing reminder that she is the product of a sexual relationship—a sexual relationship for which she, not the white father (the one who holds the power), bears the burden. The mulatta is then the evidence that contradicts the basic philosophical concept of slavery—that blacks are not human (Christian 1985, 3).

While I agree with both Walker and Christian in part, my thesis, in contrast, claims that although black women used their writing for the pleasure and sympathy of their audience, more importantly they used their works containing the foremother figure and mulatta as vehicles for social change. I maintain that black women writers portrayed the foremother figure in their writings during the late nineteenth century and early twentieth century in order to define the mulatta and her role in social change, and to subvert the stereotypical mammy. I focus on the foremother figure, which is inherent in the works of early black women writers, as a deliberate act to transform her from object to subject, and to move her from the periphery to the center. The foremother is far more important than her marginal role in the plot seems to indicate. The appeal, blame, contradiction, and tension surrounding the mulatta heroine as an individual are secondary to the role of the foremother in this literary analysis. It is the foremother and her important place in the literature of early black women writers that is central here. Also, it is the complementary foremother-mulatta heroine relationship that is critical in the individual life of the heroine and her ultimate engagement in the collective life of the black community.

The black community still struggles with cultural images that reinforce beliefs that certain groups of individuals are entitled to more or less of society's resources simply because of gender, race, and social status. These beliefs serve as the basis for class conflict and result in a form of intergroup conflict within the black community where importance is placed on light vs. dark complexion and good hair vs. bad hair (Jewell 1993, 60). Rather than emphasize the conflict, the construction of the foremother figure in early black women's writings seeks to determine the complementary elements of the relationship between the foremother and the mulatta. The foremother and mulatta seemingly existed in two different worlds and grappled with different concerns; however, discursive practices define and determine the significance of the correlation between the physically unattractive mammy—a useful vessel—and the beautiful but deficient mulatta heroine. Christian anchors the latter's deficiency in early nineteenth-century ethnologist Josiah Nott's conclusion that the mulatta was weaker and less fertile than either parent (1980, 16). The *Oxford English Dictionary* notes that the origin of the word *mulatto* is *mulo*, which means *mule*, an animal that results from mixing. The historical range of meanings noted in the *OED*, regardless of period or context, still indicates a person or thing that is judged to be less than genuine. One definition referred to anyone of mixed race, another to the mix between Negroes and Indians. Still another definition for mulatto was half-Christian. In addition to human beings, mulatto has had as its referent speckled stones, types of clay, and types of soil. In 1891, significant for the period of this study, the term "mulatto jack" referred to yellow fever. One can conclude that all references to mulatto imply some form of mixing, which presumes weakness or some variant of that which is pure.

In contrast, then, to the foremother figure, the mulatta is portrayed stereotypically as the tragic mulatta, the black female whose mother was black and powerless and whose father was white and powerful but disowns her. The tragic mulatta is the one for whom the laws were written to determine that one drop of black blood determines race. She remains a constant threat to the ideal white female. The tragic mulatta sees all the advantages of being white, and often at some point in her life is afforded the opportunity to pass and acquire an education and/or a lifestyle of material ease. But she becomes tragic when the discovery of her ancestry threatens this status and her happiness.

The foremother figure, on the other hand, occupies a place in the prescribed social depth of enslavement or employment in the home of whites. Those in power give her little consideration and perceive her as a mere dark abiding presence. She is, in fact, a persistent black female figure who possesses the emotional stability, the strength to endure, and the audacity to hope. The foremother possesses wisdom instead of education; she serves as a moral repository and naturally preserves and cherishes the culture. She is "clothed in her right mind"; that is, she is surrounded by the dominant culture, but not controlled by it to the extent that she compromises her own cultural beliefs. The phrase "clothed in my right mind," in black culture, reflects what might be called a diachronic culturally-specific change in language which originates from the King James version of the gospel of Mark 5:15: "And they come to Jesus, and see him that was possessed with the devil, and had the legion, sitting and clothed, and in his right mind: and they were afraid." While the man was possessed with the unclean spirit of the devil, the people were unsuccessful as they attempted to bind him with chains to prevent him from physically abusing himself. After Jesus commanded the unclean spirit to depart from the body of the man, the people saw him sitting and "clothed in his right mind." He had undergone a change so profound that the people were afraid. In both instances the man is in the world but not of the world. In his former state he was demonized; in his current state he is sanctified. Both states represent the extreme in that he is different from the masses. The biblical parable of the legion is much like the literary figure of the foremother, not in the manner of his revolutionary change, but in its outcome. The man possesses a spiritual awareness that sets him apart from the masses so that "the people were afraid." The foremother's spirituality sets her apart from the masses. She does not elicit fear from the masses but reverence. She therefore influences others and effects change. Historically and still today, blacks repeatedly express the words, "clothed in my right mind," in testimony and prayer in the black church. One gives thanks when he or she utters the phrase "clothed in my right mind." This utterance signifies that he or she has, at some point, experienced a spiritual change which affects how he or she now views the world. The foremother figure, therefore, in all her spiritual, emotional, moral, cultural, and physical complexities holds a central transformatory purpose as she is re-visioned in the works of black women writers.

Alice Walker advises writers to trust the experiences coming out of their own culture, use the resources of their own knowledge, feelings, and thoughts, and isolate the fantasies of others (1932a, 312). The purpose of my investigation is to isolate the myth of the stereotypical mammy and reveal how early black women writers subvert this persistent figure with the foremother figure, and then to argue that black women writers used a seemingly identical but in fact a vastly different figure than white female writers used during the late nineteenth and early twentieth centuries. Specifically, I seek answers to the following questions:

1. What is historically inherent in the construction of the stereotypical mammy image that enabled it to persist through the periods of slavery, Reconstruction, post-Reconstruction, and the Harlem Renaissance?

2. The stereotypical mammy appears to be the same in black female literature as in white female literature during the periods of slavery, Reconstruction, post-Reconstruction, and the Harlem Renaissance. Did black women writers use the stereotype to fulfill white audience expectations or did black women writers use it to subvert the stereotypical image of the black female in literature, or both?

3. What evidence is available in the language of selected primary texts that supports the idea that black women writers used the foremother figure to subvert the stereotypical mammy in order to define the mulatta heroine?

4. What character traits and aspects of behavior found in the foremother figure yield the construction of a positive image based on characteristics representative of the black culture?

The critical approach I will use to characterize the foremother figure is the re-reading and re-visioning of relevant portions of primary texts, emphasizing the analysis of speech situations and comparative character study. The purpose is to establish that the presumed stereotypical mammy portrayed in the works of black women is in fact a different representation from the black woman portrayed in the literature of white females. She is used in a similar role and occupies, on a first reading, what appears to be a minor place in the writings of black women; however, differences exist in the delineation of character, as already suggested by Barbara Christian (1985, 2). Molefi K. Asante suggests that to delineate character is not to determine authorial intent, but to 'locate' the writer; that is, a text is socially constructed; therefore, a writer always leaves some evidence of his or her attitude with the use of the language (1992, 13). In his essay entitled "Locating a Text: Implications of Afrocentric Theory," Asante clearly explains how one uses the text to make meaningful observations about the author's language use, character portrayal, and audience in order to 'locate' the author or to determine the world view of the author. I will study character portrayal and language use in the works of early white and black women writers to determine the differences that exist seemingly in their identical portrayal of the older black woman figure.

A brief example from an early white female work is Caroline Hentz's description of Aunt Kizzi in *The Planter's Northern Bride*: "ebony face, thick African lips, flattened in a broad smile . . . grunting as she picks up after the child" (1:212). The lexical items selected to describe this older black woman from the outside vary little from the repeated description of the mammy figure in other white literature. The author sees no further than the images held strongly in place by the ideology that balances features in the figure of the ideal white female with opposing features in the figure of the older black woman. In *Hagar's Daughter*, on the other hand, Pauline Hopkins sketches a portrait of Aunt Henny as a seventy-year-old, pipe-smoking "coal-black negress of kindly face" (33). One difference between the two portraits is that physical features are well-defined in Hentz and echo the well-worn descriptions of the explorers who visited Africa centuries ago. The depictions are similar but differ on the level of the lexical descriptions selected to inscribe the older black woman. Hopkins adds a further dimension when she presents Aunt Henny speaking perfect Black English in her own voice and possessing a level of common sense called wisdom as she talks about her monetary savings and the significance of home ownership: "I got one hunder' dollars up stairs 'tween the feather bed an' de mattress. . . . Can't feel de place is ourn till we's paid up. When I sees you and de chillun under your own roof, I gwine ter gib up de ghos' in peace." (175). In Hentz's words the older black woman is presented as an object. Hopkins's portrait is centered on the older black woman as a subject. She expounds on economics, ownership, and discipline. Aunt Henny possesses agency rather than passivity when she is placed in the position of subject.

In his essay, "Locating a Text . . . ," Asante applies his theory of 'location' of the writer to the work of a black male poet. I will add to work in this area by examining the discursive practices of early black women's fictional works. I will attempt to isolate the myth of the stereotypical mammy and show how the older black woman's language use subverts the myth and creates the mold for the authentic construction of the foremother. The foremother is a literary construction that is characterized by the language of the foremother figure and the language of those with whom she interacts. It is the use of meaningful language that reveals the veiled efforts of the early black woman writer to utilize a true "Afrocentric rhetoric," in the figure of the foremother. A true "Afrocentric rhetoric," according to Molefi K. Asante, is language that opposes those things that negate the cultural experiences of blacks, and is committed to the propagation of a more humanistic vision of the world (1987, 170). Specific to this literary study, the construction of the foremother figure opposes or subverts the negative image of the older black woman in the generalized figure of the stereotypical mammy. The foremother figure expresses through her own voice the imparting cultural wisdom in the texts of early black women writers. I will re-read the texts to determine the place of the foremother figure and the extent to which she influences the lives of other major and minor characters.

To further refine my analysis, I will determine through the traditional new critical textual analysis how the foremother evolves through characterization by foils as she helps to clarify the mulatta figure. The African American texts to be studied in this project are as follows: Harriet Jacobs's *Incidents in the Life of a Slave Girl Written by Herself* (1861); Frances Harper's novel *Iola Leroy or Shadows Uplifted* (1892), and her novellas *Minnie's Sacrifice* (1869), and *Trial and Triumph* (1888-89); Pauline Hopkins's *Hagar's Daughter: A Story of Southern Caste Prejudice* (1901-02), and *Of One Blood or the Hidden Self*, (1902-03); and *Jessie Fauset's There Is Confusion* (1924), *Plum*

Bun: A Novel Without a Moral (1928), *The Chinaberry Tree: A Novel of American Life* (1931), and *Comedy: American Style* (1933).

LITERATURE REVIEW

I have already referred to a number of secondary works that shed light on stereotypes of black women, some of which speak specifically to the literary portrayal of the mammy image during the nineteenth century. What follows is a brief review of the most relevant of these secondary works listed according to their reference to the portrayal of the mammy image during the nineteenth century, women writing during the nineteenth-century, and the mammy and stereotypes of blacks in general. Each review includes an assessment about how my approach adds to this discussion.

One source that provides a full discussion of the mammy stereotype in nineteenth-century literary works is *From Mammies to Militants: Domestics in Black American Literature* (1982) by Trudier Harris. She provides literary and real-life historical accounts of black women domestics. Of general interest is Harris's discussion concerning how the literary portrayal of the maid reveals whether the writer is committed to the social advancement of blacks. Of particular use to my study is Harris's claim that the black female character consistently struggles against some facet of stereotypical characterization in black male and female nineteenth and twentieth-century works. The foremother figure, then, typifies Harris's claim as it subverts the stereotypical mammy.

Another work of particular importance is Hazel Carby's *Reconstructing Womanhood: The Emergence of the Afro-American Woman Novelist* (1987). In her chapter on "Slave and Mistress: Ideologies of Womanhood under Slavery," Carby examines the nature of black womanhood in the context of assumptions about "true [white] womanhood" in the works of blacks and whites. She shows how stereotypes in literature function as a disguise for social relations. In her chapter on Nella Larsen she also offers useful ideas on the function of this mulatta as a literary device. My work differs in focus in that I examine and illuminate the language surrounding the foremother figure to establish the significance and extent of her socio-familial relationship with the mulatta heroine.

Still another work which narrows the focus of the image of the black woman in literature is Mary P. Robinson Viguerie's dissertation entitled My Dear Ol' Mammy in Southern Literature (1993). Viguerie argues that early black writers, male and female, portray the figure of the mammy in such a way that it is really an expansion of the plantation version. She believes that black writers denounce slavery and refute aspects of the stereotype, but that all versions really confirm, rather than subvert, a general conception of mammy as evidence of intertexuality. All versions have as their basis the vision of stability, home, harmony, and a rural society (17). Although Viguerie includes early black works such as Jacobs's *Incidents* and Harper's *Iola Leroy* along with early white works such as Caroline Hentz's *The Planter's Northern Bride*, my work differs from Viguerie's in that I am suggesting that there are identifiable differences between the white female writer's portrayal of the mammy and the subversive black woman writer's portrayal when one views the mammy through her language and in the context of the mulatta heroine.

In her dissertation entitled A Peculiar Motherhood: The Black Mammy Figure in American Literature and Popular Iconography, 1824-1965 (1995) Kimberly Wallace-Sanders studies how the mammy figure, which symbolized racial harmony, was transformed from a pro-slavery representation, which included all the expected physical and behavioral characteristics, to a late nineteenth-century figure representing commercialism and consumption. Of interest to my work is that Wallace-Sanders compares the mammy's relationship with the children of the white owner or employer with the relationship with her own children. Wallace-Sanders sees the stereotype as responding to audience expectations and uses visual illustration and literary dialogue in her analysis. My work differs from Wallace-Sanders in that I focus on the foremother and her relationship with the mulatta, and base my analysis on the influence of the foremother's language use in the life of the mulatta rather than on the presumed authorial intention about audience.

A more general work which relates to the period of my study is Frances Smith Foster's essay entitled "Adding Color and Contour to Early American Self-Portraitures: Autobiographical Writings of Afro-American Women," in Marjorie Pryse and Hortense J. Spillers's *Conjuring: Black Women, Fiction and Literary Tradition* (1985). Foster looks at the relationship between genre and characterization as she examines two early black female autobiographical works. She discusses how Jarena Lee and Nancy Prince illustrate new forms and styles of nineteenth-century autobiographical writing as each writer goes beyond the simple reversal of stereotypes in her form of characterization. Each writer offers a redefinition of femininity and a woman's proper place. My work, primarily on another genre, confirms Foster's in that my focus on the portrayal of the stereotypical mammy figure in the fiction of white females and the foremother figure in the literature of black women shows that black women writers of fiction certainly went beyond the mere reversal of a stereotype, as the foremother represents not simply an individual but a cultural context and a social commentary.

In *Domestic Allegories of Political Desire: The Black Heroine's Text at the Turn of the Century* (1992) Claudia Tate does not speak on the particular topic of subverting stereotypical figures, but generally on the topic of reconstructing first audiences. Since audience acts as a constraint, Tate discusses how the texts of white antebellum female literature celebrate the consummation of the orderly household as a sign of a moral society, while the texts of black women writers mourn the violation of black womanhood, maternity, family, and home. Amelia E. Johnson's *The Hazeley Family* (1894) and *Clarence and Corinne or God's Way* (1890) are examples of late nineteenth-century texts which mourn the violation of family and home. My work will add to Tate's work in that I will attempt to show that despite these violations, the language of the foremother uncovers the positive and strengthening relationship that exists between the older black woman and the mulatta heroine and among black folks in general. Early black women writers reveal that despite the ever-present oppressive conditions, the constraints of audience expectations, the ever-looming negative images, and the seemingly impossible situations in the home, community, and society of black folks, there are ties that bind. I will project the spirit of the language of the foremother as an abiding element of the tradition of black women writers.

A final source which addresses issues related to the period of my study is Frances Smith Foster's *Written by Herself: Literary Production by African American Women, 1746-1892* (1993). Foster discusses the works of early African American women writers and some of the elements that constitute the tradition. She comments on a work by each African American woman writer mentioned in my study through Pauline Hopkins. In her commentary Foster notes that Harper was aggressive in her attempt to portray the African American perspective through characterization and style of language. It is through such characterization and pragmatics of language that I contextualize my more specific investigation of the foremother and her relationship with the mulatta.

A secondary source which looks at the mammy figure and stereotypes of black women in general is Elizabeth Schultz's essay "'Free in Fact and at Last': The Image of the Black Woman in Black American Fiction," in Marlene Springer's edited collection, *What Manner of Woman: Essays on English and American Life and Literature* (1977). Schultz discusses later black women writers such as Zora Neale Hurston, Kristin Hunter, and Margaret Walker, who in *Jubilee* looks back to the period of this study. Schultz discusses how twentieth-century black women writers have redefined blackness, beauty, and womanhood according to standards other than the white ideal. Schultz says that black women writers have inverted the image of ugliness and found beauty and strength in blackness. My work shows how early black women writers already were redefining the stereotypical mammy image, specifically in characterization through language use.

Discursive practices in the form of remembrance enables Veta Smith Tucker to examine the mammy in her dissertation entitled Reconstructing Mammy: Fictive Reinterpretations of Mammy's Role in the Slave Community and Image in American Culture (1994). Tucker studies representations of the mammy figure in the historical novels of contemporary black women writers to show how they oppose the sentimental image constructed in early white literature. She examines the figure of the slave woman in the works of contemporary writers Sherley Anne Williams, Toni Morrison, and Octavia Butler to show how these writers have corrected, developed, and transformed the construct of mammy. My work adds to Tucker's, as it did to Schultz's, in that I focus on the early writings of the black woman and her presentation of the foremother figure. My work will conclude with a brief discussion of a few selected works of contemporary black women writers, but only to suggest that the foremother figure undergoes change, yet remains in the literature as an inheritance from the nineteenth century.

DEFINITIONS

As I examine a representative sample of works written by black women during slavery, Reconstruction/post-Reconstruction, and the Harlem

Renaissance, I will use words repeatedly in this text which may require definition:

Foremother Figure—an older black woman who acts as a moral repository, preserves and cherishes the black culture, possesses wisdom and intense spirituality, and is instrumental in defining the mulatta heroine through language use in black women's literature.

Negro, Black, African American—used interchangeably as the reference changes over time; people of African descent.

Mulatto, Mulatta—masculine and feminine spellings for an individual with mixed heritage—black and white.

Woman, female—generally used for blacks.

Lady, female—generally used for whites.

OUTLINE

This study consists of a total of seven chapters. Following this introductory chapter, Chapter Two will present a portrait of the stereotypical mammy figure in the literature of white females. Included in Chapter Two will be analyses of Harriet Beecher Stowe's *Uncle Tom's Cabin* [1852] (1966), Caroline Hentz's *The Planter's Northern Bride* (1854), Kate Chopin's *The Awakening* (1899) (1993), and three of Kate Chopin's short stories, "Beyond the Bayou," "A No Account Creole," and "La Belle Zoraïde."

Chapter Three offers a re-reading of relevant portions of Harriet Jacobs's [Linda Brent's] *Incidents in the Life of a Slave Girl* [1861] (1987), in which the foremother figure is Aunt Nancy and the mulatta heroine is Linda Brent. Chapter Four consists of an examination of Frances Harper's *Iola Leroy or Shadows Uplifted* (1892), in which the foremother figure is Aunt Linda and the mulatta heroine is Iola Leroy. I will also examine newly discovered works by Frances Harper entitled *Minnie's Sacrifice* (1869), and *Trial and Triumph* (1888-89). In Chapter Six I will examine Pauline Hopkins's *Hagar's Daughter: A Story of Southern Caste Prejudice* (1901-1902), in which the foremother figure is Aunt Henny and the mulatta heroine is Hagar. I will also examine Pauline Hopkins's *Of One Blood or the Hidden Self* (1902-03), where the foremother figure is Aunt Hannah and the mulatta heroine is Dianthe Lusk. Chapter Six looks at Jessie Redmon Fauset's

Plum Bun: A Novel Without a Moral (1928), in which the foremother figure is Hetty and the mulatta heroine is Angela Murray. I will also examine additional works by Jessie Redmon Fauset entitled *There Is Confusion* (1924), *The Chinaberry Tree: A Novel of American Life* (1931), and *Comedy: American Style* (1933).

Chapter Seven concludes my discussion of the treatment of the foremother figure in selected writings of early black women writers of fiction and looks to the future. Using the textual evidence gathered in this study, I will determine how the black woman writer located the foremother figure in her texts based on language use and specify the differences between the black woman's representation of the foremother figure and the white woman's representation of the stereotypical mammy figure. In this concluding chapter I will offer implications for future research and discuss how the foremother figure has been inherited in the print media of later black women writers, as Jewell has documented the presence of this figure in the electronic media today. The foremother in later black women's literature emerges, for example, as Nanny in Zora Neale Hurston's *Their Eyes Were Watching God* [1937] (1990), Lutie's grandmother in Ann Petry's *The Street* (1946), and Miranda and Abigail in Gloria Naylor's *Mama Day* (1988).

The older black woman persists and resists. As the foremother figure she persists and performs socio-cultural functions in the works of early black women writers. As the foremother figure she resists the myths, the assumptions, and the ideology behind the stereotypical mammy in the works of early white women writers.

CHAPTER 2

The Mammy in Early White Female Writers
Harriet Beecher Stowe, Caroline Lee Hentz, and Kate Chopin

Harriet Beecher Stowe, Caroline Lee Hentz, and Kate Chopin are representative of nineteenth-century white women writers who produced works that reflect a range in their portrayal of the black female character—a range that includes clear examples of the older black woman in the role of the stereotypical mammy. This chapter will determine the basis on which each mammy figure is delineated within the context of the ideal white female by drawing attention to the language of the narrator, the white mistress, the minor character, and the mammy figure herself, as well as the absence of the language. Both Stowe's *Uncle Tom's Cabin* (1852) and Hentz's *The Planter's Northern Bride* (1854) were published prior to the Civil War. Stowe writes from the anti-slavery and Hentz from the pro-slavery perspective. Chopin integrates race, gender, and class issues in her short stories, "La Belle Zoraïde (1894), "A No Account Creole" (1894), and "Beyond the Bayou" (1894), and in her novel, *The Awakening* (1899), which were published long after the Civil War. Chopin published during a decade when black female literary works flourished.

In the great expansion of white women's writing and publishing in the nineteenth century, the popular domestic novel, according to Jane Tompkins represents an effort to reorganize culture from the woman's point of view. Domestic and sentimental novels dominated white women's writings during the nineteenth century and were so widespread that male-dominated criticism categorized women's works separately in contrast to their own. Some common descriptive contrasts were light "feminine" versus tough-minded intellectual treatises, and domestic chattiness versus serious thinking. Nathaniel Hawthorne voiced the most memorable contrastive commentary on nineteenth-century white women writers in a letter to his publisher in 1855. He referred to white women writers as that "damned mob of scribbling women," presumably in contrast to a few intellectual giants such as himself (Tompkins 1985, 83).

Because many nineteenth-century women writers focussed on home and familial relationships as centers of meaningful activity, their scholarly efforts were minimized; nevertheless, they maintained their focus on the home and produced works that reflected their view of the world and those who participated in their world. The perspectives and periods of publication differ for the writers considered here—Stowe, Hentz, and Chopin; however, their works reveal more similarities than differences in the treatment of the older black woman in the context of the ideal white female. The early white woman writer may not have perceived her place as one of domination and control, but the literature reveals that she assumes the binary views of superior and inferior, strength and weakness, at all levels of society including the home. Jewell says that according to the prevailing ideology, one group must dominate another group. A system of domination breeds competition, and competition serves as an incentive for production (3), that is, work and responsibility. Elements of the system of domination that result in some form of production channeled through work and responsibility emerge in the literature of early white women writers. It is important to note how these elements relate to the ideal white female and the stereotypical mammy figure, whose origins are associated with labor. Upon re-reading works by Harriet Beecher Stowe, Carolyn Lee Hentz, and Kate Chopin, it is important to observe how this representative group of white women writers reflect similarities and differences in the literary portrayal of the stereotypical mammy, especially during the nineteenth century, when there was uncritical acceptance of stereotypes (Prenshaw 1993, 82). It is also important to heed Nina Baym's warning that contemporary scholarship fails to distinguish between earlier and later parts of the nineteenth century and instead treats the period as a single block, even though situations were clearly different for women in general (1978, 313). Using Stowe's *Uncle Tom's Cabin* (1852) and Chopin's *The Awakening* (1899) as my middle and latter-century text with the focus on the portrayal of the older black woman in the context of the white female, I see the former as a well-integrated mainstay in the household—the center of patriarchal rule, helping to define the ideal white female. Toward the latter part of the century, I see the older black woman as a presence that is still easily identified by her household and care-giving duties in the white home, yet she is more of a presence whose occasional sass and assertiveness are veiled and muted. She occupies a place in the white household but not the integral position that she was portrayed to have held during the middle of the nineteenth century. Yet, she remains.

AUNT CHLOE, AUNT DINAH AND MAMMY IN *UNCLE TOM'S CABIN*

Harriet Beecher Stowe's *Uncle Tom's Cabin* (1852) inscribes three mammy figures whose correlation with the white female results in characterizations reflected in forms of work and responsibility. Christian says of Stowe's characterization that the Negro is a dramatic focal character rather than a comic minor character (1980, 21) because feminine qualities are assigned to both male and female Negro characters. Abolitionists viewed these feminine qualities as superior rather than inferior because these were humane qualities that many whites lacked. Based on a first reading and Christian's seemingly positive criticism, one could locate the writer in abolitionism and easily disregard other significant factors associated with this dramatic focal characterization. Christian reveals, however, that this quality of feminization parallels servility; thus dramatic focal characterization is not necessarily a superior or positive character portrayal, but fitting for the Negro, whether male or female. Similar to Christian, Ducksworth finds that the author's antislavery sentiments, though full of righteous condemnation, lack notions of racial equality (1994, 205), even though religion, which assumes spiritual egalitarianism, is used as a motif for her message of sympathy. Such contradictions of course, are not unusual among white abolitionists. Yarborough, too, finds that although Stowe sympathized with the slave, her commitment to challenging the claim of black inferiority was undermined by her own endorsement of racial stereotypes (1986, 47). An example of this endorsement is evident in the narrator's description of the stereotypical figure, Aunt Chloe:

> A round, black, shining face is hers, so glossy as to suggest the idea
> that she might have been washed over with white of eggs . . . . Her
> whole plump countenance beams with satisfaction and contentment
> from under her well-starched checked turban . . . the first cook of the
> neighborhood, as Aunt Chloe was universally held and acknowledged
> to be. A cook she certainly was, in the very bone and centre of her
> soul (31).

The narrator couches the stereotypical element of contentment in the
description of physical features and defines Aunt Chloe innately as a
cook, hence a servant. A close reading further reveals that the language
of the stereotypical mammy complements this tone of condescension
reflected in the voice of the narrator. It is only Aunt Chloe who refers to
herself as mammy, and it is only Aunt Chloe who refers to her sons as
niggers when she says, "Here you, Mose and Pete! get out de way, you
niggers! Get away, Polly, honey,—mammy'll give her baby somefin,
by and by" (33). Her language provides further role-and self-
identification when Aunt Chloe refers to Mrs. Shelby in saying, "I can't
do nothin' with ladies in de kitchen" (36). In a similar passage later in
the St. Clare household in response to Miss Ophelia's rearranging the
kitchen, Dinah, another mammy figure in the novel, says, "if dat ar de
way dem northern ladies do dey an't ladies no how . . ." and "I don't
want ladies round a henderin' . . ." (229). In both instances the language
confirms the myth of contentment in the work role in which each older
black woman is cast. Both characters express dissatisfaction when the
white mistress attempts to change the configuration of their routine or
attempts to enter their work space—the space that defines who they are
as a dark presence that occupies a realm on the periphery of someone
else's center. Their relative autonomy is both created and circumscribed
by the power hierarchy. Grumbling over interference from the mistress
is tolerable insofar as it confirms the mammy's subservient status.

   A typical mammy, Aunt Chloe is portrayed as one whose vision is
skewed by the oppressive institution of slavery. When her emotional
rebelliousness assumes more serious proportions when her family is
broken up, she still remains fatalistic. She holds that the next generation
will be bound by the same systemic pattern of separation of family
regardless of industry or loyalty. To her children she says, "ye'll live to
see yer husband sold, or mebbe be sold yerself " (111). Although Aunt
Chloe's heartbreak and hopelessness are portrayed sympathetically
when the family prepares for Uncle Tom's departure, the narrator in her

omniscience nevertheless objectifies and stereotypes the Negro when she says "that all the instinctive affections of that race are peculiarly strong. Their local attachments are very abiding. They are not naturally daring and enterprising, but home-loving and affectionate" (109). Aunt Chloe's bitterness and despair are thus passed over, relegated condescendingly to a racial stereotype of the other. Moving immediately to a practical hope, Aunt Chloe can imagine only an extension of her work productivity—baking—as a way to purchase Tom's freedom (277).

In general black characters in *Uncle Tom's Cabin* served the writer's abolitionist purpose and at the same time fulfilled white audience expectations. Ducksworth suggests that today's reading audience asks what the characters represent and how they function in the novel (1994, 214). It is obvious that Stowe envisions no beauty in female blackness since none of her dark-skinned women characters possesses pleasant features. Ducksworth points out that this presumption is confirmed by her depiction of quadroons laughing at dark-skinned blacks (1994, 231). Alice Walker refers to such a response as colorism, defined as prejudicial or preferential treatment of same-race people based solely on their color (1983, 290). This action divides people of the same race. Strengthening a system of hierarchy, domination, and control requires weakening the ties that bind a people. To define whiteness as the ideal accomplishes both. Again, Aunt Chloe's reference to herself as mammy and to her children as niggers, and a quadroon's derision of dark-skinned blacks reveal the perpetuation of inferiority among blacks. Negative language flows from the mouths of these fellow black characters as profusely and naturally as it does from white characters. Such language confirms that an oppressive system is effective when its victims begin to see themselves through the eyes of the oppressor. The oppressed group fulfills the role expectations defined by the dominant group. Stowe's *Uncle Tom's Cabin* supports the view that the institution of slavery or legalized subjugation is bad, but also that the white race is generally superior to the black race (even if an individual such as Tom may be morally superior to an individual white man, such as Mr. Shelby). This belief is clearly inscribed in portrayals of the white mistress and in her correlate, the stereotypical mammy.

The white mistress is used as the female standard based on her behavioral characteristics as exemplified in the character of Miss Ophelia and especially Marie St. Clare. Miss Ophelia, a northerner, believes—paternalistically—that the slave owner is responsible for his slave's behavior and will be held accountable before God (194), just as the slave owner is responsible for his own behavior and will be held accountable before God. As in her beliefs, she is described according to her habits of order, method, and exactness. She holds in contempt and abomination anything of a contrary character, such as Topsy (174-75). Such an attitude characterizes those who participate in the construction and maintenance of stereotypical images. Anything or anyone perceived to be different from oneself can then be relegated to the "other." The "other" is objectified; it is scrutinized and judged from a distance. One is thus justified in treating the "other" differently because it is defined differently.

An example of such objectification lies in the cases of womanhood and motherhood. This objectification of the "other" is exemplified above all in Marie St. Clare's perception of the slave in general. She views all slaves as children (191) and makes every effort to maintain the superior-inferior hierarchy, which she believes neither the northern white female nor the southern white male fully comprehends (191-92). Stowe is clearly critical of the Southern mistress mentality when she characterizes Marie St. Clare's general and specific views regarding her slaves. With her southern mistress mentality, Marie objectifies in particular her slave, Mammy, when she contends that Mammy could not love her dirty children as she (Marie) loves her own daughter, Eva: "Mammy could n't have the feelings that I should. It 's a different thing altogether,—of course, it is,—and yet St. Clare pretends not to see it. And just as if Mammy could love her little dirty babies as I love Eva!" (191). Marie St. Clare views Mammy as incapable of a mother's love. Marie's perspective places Mammy outside the realm of not only motherhood, but womanhood, since a characteristic of womanhood is to be motivated largely by emotion. This link between womanhood and the capability to feel and to empathize is confirmed earlier when Mrs. Shelby is accused of allowing herself to feel. An argument ensues while Mr. and Mrs. Shelby are discussing the sale of Eliza's child, Harry. Of note is Mrs. Shelby's use of the word "woman" rather than "lady" in response to Mr. Shelby's accusation: "you allow yourself to feel too much." Mrs. Shelby responds, "Feel too much! Am not I a woman—a mother?" (84). Because of its use in this context, the term "woman" is indeed more meaningful and more substantial than "lady." The word "woman" clearly connotes life and nurturance in its connection to motherhood. "Lady," on the other hand, stereotypical in itself, bears the connotation of a porcelain figure, incapable of serving any purpose other than adornment or accessory. The superficiality of the alabaster lady image emerges again when Senator Bird urges his wife to repress her emotions. The narrator describes Mrs. Bird as "a timid, blushing little woman, about four feet in height, and with mild blue eyes, and a peach-blow complexion, and the gentlest, sweetest voice in the world" (91). During their discussion of the Fugitive Slave Law Senator Bird says, "we must n't suffer our feelings to run away with our judgment; we must put aside our private feelings" (93). This is yet another instance in Stowe's *Uncle Tom's Cabin* that reveals that the preservation of the white female porcelain facade is controlled mainly by the props of patriarchy.

The stereotypical mammy in her role of mother and worker is not admonished for her outward expression of feelings because such unrestrained expressions enact the opposite emotional response from that imposed upon the white lady. While Eliza tells her story of escape, "Mrs. Bird had her face fairly hidden in her pocket-handkerchief; and old Dinah, with tears streaming down her black, honest face, was ejaculating, 'Lord have mercy on us' with all the fervor of a camp-meeting" (97-98). The stereotypical mammy is characterized by extremes, yet she is perceived to possess feelings at a lower level than the white lady, for she is made to endure the agony of separation from her own husband and children, as cited earlier in the characterization of Mammy. Marie St. Clare, for example, tells Miss Ophelia that Mammy is "smooth and respectful, but she 's selfish at heart. Now, she will never be done fidgeting and worrying about that husband of hers" (186). The stereotypical mammy's role as wife holds little significance when her reason for being is perceived as merely to render personal services for the white mistress and her family, and to serve as a correlate in order to maintain the ideal white female image.

It is not only the stereotypical mammy's physical and behavioral features, but even her family life that is depicted as vastly different from that of her correlate, the ideal white female. Regarding the contrasts between Aunt Chloe and Mrs. Shelby and old Dinah and Mrs. Bird, Stowe reveals how black and white women function within their separate families. Both are like magnets, holding their very distinct cultures together (Ducksworth 219). Stowe constructs obvious contrasts not only between Mrs. Shelby and Aunt Chloe, but even between their dwellings. Mrs. Shelby's dwelling is called "the house," while Aunt Chloe's is called "snug territories" (30). Inscribed in the text also is an imposed hierarchy among the slaves: "The evening meal at the house is over, and Aunt Chloe, who presided over its preparation as 'head cook,' has left to 'inferior officers' in the kitchen the business of clearing away and washing dishes . . ." (30). Again, Stowe's selection of lexical items is representative of her world view. As in the society at large the writer sees hierarchy, domination, and competitive individualism as a way of life even at the very core of family life—the home. Ironically the center of the home, the kitchen, is supervised by the mammy figure as Stowe, with mockery and condescension, inscribes Aunt Chloe with a level of authority in the hierarchy as "head cook" over the "inferior officers."

Again, the aspect of hierarchical portrayals most significant for this study in Stowe's *Uncle Tom's Cabin* is the contrast between the ideal white female and the stereotypical mammy. The character whose name is Mammy is described as a middle-aged mulatta with a respectable appearance (181). Marie St. Clare's child, Eva, loves Mammy unconditionally. Mammy's severe headaches are minimized and altogether disregarded by others, yet the reader knows of her suffering because of Eva's empathy. Marie St. Clare's physical and mental ailments are maximized. She voices her complaints so frequently that everyone knows of her condition (184). Further, Marie blames her slaves for her ill health. She thinks Mammy to be selfish because Mammy sleeps soundly and is thus unaware of Marie's discomfort (185). Marie judges Mammy by what she expects as an acceptable level of production. She sees her servants in general as grown children and describes them as stupid, unreasonable, childish wretches (191). Marie exercises the freedom to define; thus the implication of her superiority is clear.

This implied superior nature of the white female goes beyond the individual to the family and ultimately to society. According to Ducksworth *Uncle Tom's Cabin* portrays the white woman not only to be superior, but to possess strength of character like a powerful field of light which is used to guide and uplift her male partner and her sons (219). Although this characterization does not fit Marie St. Clare, whom Stowe treats as an unworthy exception, both Mrs. Shelby and Mrs. Bird exemplify the ideal white female who voices her view on slavery and pricks the consciousness of her male companion, even though her words are tempered by the constraints of patriarchy so as not to blur the boundaries of the portrayal of her superior nature. Even though the white female, Marie St. Clare, does not possess in reality the superior nature she thinks she has and that is reflected in Mrs. Shelby and Mrs. Bird, she is portrayed to be superior in status to the black woman regardless of her moral disposition as a white female. The older black woman, on the other hand,—as represented by Chloe—is merely a force which supports her child-like black male and her uncouth sons. Ducksworth refers to the stark contrast between Stowe's black and white mothers when they reprimand their children. During dinner in her home, Aunt Chloe speaks to her sons with an overall tone of intolerance, "'Oh, go long, will ye?'" and "giving now and then a kick, in a general way under the table." She sternly warns, "'Better mind yerselves or I'll take ye down a button-hole lower, when Mas'r George is gone. Get along wid ye!' she said, pushing away their woolly heads" (37). On the other hand, the narrator describes Mrs. Bird's interaction with her children in a tone of poetic loving tolerance: "ever and anon mingling admonitory remarks to a number of frolicsome juveniles, who were effervescing in all those modes of untold gambol and mischief that have astonished mothers ever since the flood" (90).

Stowe's range of characterization of the black female extends beyond the stark contrasts suggested by Ducksworth. In fact, Stowe portrays heart-wrenching scenes of black mother-child relationships in the portraits of Eliza and Harry when Eliza risks their lives while crossing the Ohio River on ice (72). A similar portrayal consists of Susan and Emmeline, mother and daughter respectively, as they await the wretched experience of the auction block and Susan agonizes over the curse of black beauty within the confines of enslavement (355).

Amid this range of sympathetic portrayals, however, remains the perpetuation of stereotypical images consistent in the correlation between the black female as mammy and the white female as mistress. The white mistress portrayed in the works of early white women writers participates in the perpetuation of images that stereotype physical features and predict behavior, especially when the behavior relates to work and responsibility. The stereotypical mammy and the ideal white lady are consistently portrayed together in the context of work and responsibility.

As noted in *Uncle Tom's Cabin*, work and responsibility play a major role in maintaining hierarchy, domination, competitive individualism, and thus production. Work and responsibility are also used as activities that distinguish and identify. Drew Gilpin Faust, like Barbara Christian, stresses that the white female's identity depended on having others perform life's menial tasks. Faust learns from primary sources such as letters and diaries that one white female, after securing a slave to resume her household duties, stated, "she had taken the cooking and we are all ladies again. . . ." Another complained that her husband did not know how much a woman's happiness depended on good servants (1996, 77). "Lady" and "work" are perceived to be incongruent; where one exists the other cannot. In Stowe's *Uncle Tom's Cabin*, two of the stereotypical mammies, Dinah and Aunt Chloe, communicate the notion that if one is classified as lady, one cannot function in the kitchen. Faust contends that most white women saw themselves as incompetent to manage their slaves, and most slaves shared their mistress's views of their own incompetence (56-57). This is clearly shown in black female slave narratives such as *The History of Mary Prince* (1831), and *Incidents in the Life of a Slave Girl Written by Herself* (1861). In the former narrative Mrs. Woods repeatedly threatened to order Mary Prince flogged because of her sass. It was seldom that she followed through in her threat. In the latter narrative Harriet Jacobs characterizes the incompetence of Mrs. Flint as incapable of running her home while Jacobs's Aunt Nancy is in jail. Not only is this incompetence inscribed in early black women's works, but in early white women's works like Caroline Lee Hentz's *The Planter's Northern Bride.*

PERFECTING MAMMY IN HENTZ'S *THE PLANTER'S NORTHERN BRIDE*

The complexity of white and black female relations is more revealing in the pro-slavery novel of Caroline Lee Hentz, *The Planter's Northern Bride* (1854). Kizzie serves as a stereotypical mammy correlate to the ideal white female, Eula, exhibiting the expected embellished physical and loyal behavioral characteristics while uncovering some of the tension that exists in this relationship. Crissy provides the stereotypical mammy characteristic of loyalty as the correlate to Ildegerte. But Hentz magnifies the portraits of Aunt Dicey and Aunt Dilsey, who take loyalty and submissiveness to new depths. The complexity of the white and black female relationship will never be entirely revealed, but as noted in my Introduction and in Stowe's *Uncle Tom's Cabin*, the white female must maintain the black female presence in her sphere to keep her own identity intact, while a tension forever exists between the two females. Hentz's work reveals a relational tension not only as an outgrowth of work and responsibility couched in a patriarchal ideology, but also as a result of northern and southern ideological contrasts as Eula struggles to establish the superior-inferior hierarchy expected of a southern slave-holding mistress. Hentz includes a meaningful scene in *The Planter's Northern Bride* that depicts the variable nature of the relationship between the white mistress and mammy figure prior to the advent of the Civil War. Eula speaks to Kizzie as one would to a sister or a friend when Kizzie prepares to attend a Sunday evening church service:

> "Did you think of going to church to-night, Kizzie? Little Russell is so unwell I would rather you would not leave me. I have a bad headache myself, also."
>
> "La, missus! there is nothing the matter with him, just wakeful; that's all. He'll go to sleep directly."
>
> "I do not feel able to take care of him to-night, Kizzie. I want you to stay."
>
> "Won't Netty do, missus? . . ."
>
> "Netty has no experience, and I am sure the child is sick. . . ." She did not want Kizzie to see how much she was wounded by her reluctance to fulfil [sic] a positive duty (2:139).

More important than Eula's dependence on Kizzie is her seeming reluctance to insist upon Kizzie's remaining and taking care of the child. Eula's language suggests that she is asking a friend for a favor and is disappointed by the negative response.

Yet another dimension of this complex relationship is fear. Faust describes one white woman who talked about how her fears were aroused when her husband was absent from the plantation because of his participation in the Civil War. She recalls that "there was the fear . . . dark, boding, oppressive and altogether hateful . . ." (60). Eula experiences a similar foreboding upon first visiting her husband's plantation:

> Eula gazed with a kind of fascination on the dark procession, as one after another, men, women, and children, passed along to the gin house to deposit their burdens. It seemed as if she were watching the

progress of a great eclipse, and that soon she would be enveloped in total darkness. She was a mere speck of light, in the midst of shadows. How easy it would be to extinguish her! She recollected all the horrible stories she had heard of negro insurrections, and thought what an awful thing it was to be at the mercy of so many slaves, on that lonely plantation (2:33).

This text exemplifies Toni Morrison's contention that the need by whites to deal with internal fears and to rationalize external exploitation resulted in a construction of darkness, otherness, alarm, and desire, which Morrison calls American Africanism. She explains that suppressed and repressed darkness became objectified in American literature as an Africanist persona (1992, 38-39). Morrison's insight is borne out in another scene in Caroline Hentz's *The Planter's Northern Bride* when Eula sees her husband, Moreland, as "an angel of light surrounded by spirits of darkness, and, knowing that he was defended by the breastplate of righteousness, she was assured of his safety as well as his power" (2:200). Eula confirms the myth that the white male who participates in the system of patriarchy is symbolic of the larger-than-life white male who existed during biblical times. Hentz's choice of reference more importantly portrays the white male as one who is endowed with the light of Christ in contrast to the shadow of Satan. Scriptural use of "breastplate of righteousness" connotes a protective shield against evil—the dark abiding presence—the Africanist persona.

This tension between blacks and whites in general most assuredly made an impact on the white female's perception of the black female in ways that emerge in later literature, especially when relational hierarchies began to be disrupted by the Civil War. Some white females came to see the black female as faithful friend and servant, as suggested in Hentz's pro-slavery work, but also as protector. For some older black women, then, work and responsibility later took on the added dimension of protection.

Although work and responsibility along with the identity that results from domination and control are melded into relational structures that call for redefinition, the superior-inferior presumption still permeates the society at all levels. Hentz's work consists of numerous correlations between the ideal white female and the stereotypical mammy. The major correlations lie between Eula and Aunt Kizzie, and Ildegerte and Crissy. Eula is described as wife and mother but still having a virginal innocence: "Though a wife and mother, she retained the expression of child-like, virgin innocence, which gave her the similitude of a vestal in the white-robed village choir; and this expression was the mirror of her soul" (2:124). Aunt Kizzie, on the other hand, is described with "her ebony face shining like the sun, and her thick African lips flattened in the broad smile that parts them" (1:212-13). Aunt Kizzie is nurse, seamstress, mammy, and submistress (1:212-13); the latter indicates that she possesses some level of authority in the hierarchy of work and responsibility. Crissy, too, is so devoted to Moreland's sister, Ildegerte, that, unlike Stowe's Mammy, willingly and readily, she leaves her husband and children in order to attend to Ildegerte and her sick husband, Richard, as she resolves, "'You go, I go; Mars. Richard sick, I nuss him; take care of you. Never mind Jim and the children. Leave 'em to Lord Almighty'" (1:222). Each black female figure possesses the physical features, the behavioral features, and work activities of the stereotypical mammy.

Descending to the depths of more extreme stereotype is Hentz's depiction of Aunt Kizzie's mother, Aunt Dicey, a contented slave who serves as an example for the others:

> An old Aunt Dicey is found in almost every large household establishment at the South. The old family nurse, often the tutelary genius of three generations, the faithful servant, who had devoted the vigour of her youth and energies of her womanhood to her master's interest, and to his children's service (1:233).

She is simple-hearted and pious, but now old and infirm. Aunt Dicey lives in what Hentz describes as a comfortable dwelling similar to Stowe's description of Aunt Chloe's "snug territories," both, naturally, on the plantation. Aunt Dicey is the one to whom all the slaves pay respect and reverence (1:232-33). Similar to Aunt Dicey, but the most stereotypical of the four stereotypical mammy figures, is Aunt Dilsey, who is described as a "most ancient and honorable matron of the establishment" (2:36). The impact of this mammy figure's language is great because it occurs while she is upon her death bed. Aunt Dilsey is prepared to depart from the corporeal state of respected elder to the spiritual state of African ancestor. Her language, however, reflects the effectiveness of a lifetime of domination—the domination of one culture over another. She says to Moreland, "'Oh! massa! 'spose you don't know poor Dilsey when you git to heben, 'cause she'll be beautiful, white angel den'" (2:52). Aunt Dilsey's view reflects a literal concept of the Christian faith. She believes that she will be changed from a corporeal to a spiritual state upon her death. Most important is that Aunt Dilsey reflects the Christian teaching of her white teachers, for she perceives the godly, the spiritual, the celestial to be white. To her people she says:

> "Yes! brudders and sisters!" she cried clapping her cold, feeble hands, "rejoice that ye eber hearn of de Lord Jesus and de blessed herarter. If we'd all staid in de heathen land, where all de black folks come from, we'd neber known noting 'bout heben, noting 'bout de hebenly 'deemer or de golden streets of de new Jerusalem. Tink of dat, if Satin eber tempt you to leave good massa and missus" (2:53).

Aunt Dilsey's sermonic discourse complements the pro-slavery message that the institution of slavery is paternal, protective, and based on Christian ethics.

The mammy figure is clearly established in Hentz in the forms of Aunt Dilsey, Aunt Dicey, Kizzie, and Crissy. Their construction permits contrast through direct discourse in expressions that reinforce the notions of the superiority of whites and the correctness of slavery. They are permitted to speak in their own variety of the language, yet their language is usurped by an early white female proslavery author to express hegemonic views and confirm stereotypical behavior. These characters' reverence for whiteness is depicted in Kizzie's loyal, child-like manner, Crissy's voluntary disruption of her own family ties, Aunt Dicey's reverence for white superiority, and Aunt Dilsey's aligning the white race with the Divine. A most significant aspect of Hentz's portrayal is the characteristic of old age ascribed to Aunt Dicey and Aunt Dilsey. To weave the ideology of proslavery through the language of the significant elder figure of the slave community is a powerful narrative strategy to promote the status quo and perpetuate a system of institutional hegemony.

CHOPIN'S SHORT STORY AND NOVEL PORTRAITS

During the latter part of the nineteenth century and early twentieth century the portrayal of the older black woman still conveys contentment with the status quo. As political and social situations change, domestic situations change. The stereotypical mammy figure laboring in the white household under the oppressive system of slavery evolved into the colored or Negro female domestic servant rendering services far below cost in the white household, where her work and responsibility still fall under the authority of the white female. Because the black female is a component of the social context, she is a constant figure in the literature. Her presence is meaningful whether she speaks or not. Trudier Harris points out that a peculiar and most degrading aspect of domestic service is the requisite of invisibility. A maid draped in invisibility is devoid of the power to cause trouble or disturb the status quo (1982, 12). Contradiction, however, surrounds the narrative strategy that silences a figure to the point of invisibility, yet permits that figure repeatedly to emerge. The ultimate silence would be the complete erasure of the black female image. Apparently presence in utter silence is more meaningful than absence.

Near the end of the nineteenth century, Chopin's work shows constructions of the dark abiding presence of blacks generally and the mammy and domestic servant figures specifically. Her style is to show that blacks are denied voice. Birnbaum suggests that the white female's struggle to use her own voice and to express her own desires silences the black female voice. Anyone over whom the white female has control cannot be realized in the language of the text (1995, 322). The correlation between the two is still racialized. The stereotypical black female acts as a correlate to the ideal white female because the black female's nonverbal presence is meaningful for the white female's verbal presence.

"La Belle Zoraïde" (1894)

Per Seyersted alludes to Kate Chopin's authorial presence when he points out that she is interested in human characteristics more than racial issues and that she is a detached observer; therefore, her own views are never imposed on the reader. Seyersted argues that Chopin never advocated social change in her works; nevertheless, he admits that in the short story "La Belle Zoraïde" Chopin reveals some level of condemnation of slavery. In "La Belle Zoraïde" Chopin permits the mammy figure, Manna-Loulou, to tell a story about a white mistress, Madame Delarivière, who forbids her mulatta slave, la belle Zoraïde, to marry the very black Negro slave, le beau Mézor. The mistress ultimately sends la belle Zoraïde's newborn to a distant neighbor. It appears that Seyersted, just as the white mistress and listener, Madame Delisle, misses the message of the story told by Manna-Loulou.

Seyersted credits Chopin's effort to denounce slavery because she shows Madame Delisle pitying the child who was snatched from her slave mother. Ever looming, however, is a system that allows one human being to have total control over another human being's life because the system demands that one group dominate while another group submit to its domination. Manna-Loulou communicates this in her story; however, the white mistress, Madame Delisle, envisions only a minute component of a massive and pervasive system of domination, so she responds with the fleeting emotions expected during a bedtime story ritual. If this story had infiltrated her heart and her mind, then Madame Delisle would have been able to see with understanding the destructive nature of a system of domination. She would have responded with outrage followed by action rather than pity followed by inaction.

Madame Delisle's cognitive impairment is paralleled by the narrator's visual impairment, which is revealed in the generalized description of Manna-Loulou's physical and behavioral characteristics. Manna-Loulou is described as "black as night" and "the old negress" (303). In contrasting images of physical beauty as white the narrator says that "the old negress had already bathed her mistress's pretty white feet and kissed them lovingly, one, then the other. She brushed her mistress's beautiful hair that was as soft and shining as satin . . . and began gently to fan Madame Delisle" (303). Behaviorally, she is portrayed at the depths of subservience, yet her story of Zoraïde reveals that she is all too aware of the system that dominates and controls her life. Given this awareness, why does she seem to adore her mistress's white beauty, even her feet? Anna Elfenbein credits Chopin for revealing the extent to which oppressed people are shaped by the stereotypes applied to them (118). In each of Chopin's representative works selected for this study, Chopin reveals behavior associated with her black female character that is consistent with the subservient stereotype; thus she is obedient in "La Belle Zoraïde," even while telling a subversive tale, silent in "A No Account Creole," and loyal in "Beyond the Bayou."

"A No Account Creole" (1894)

In Chopin's short story "A No Account Creole" blacks are easily silenced. Blacks in general are figuratively silenced through a narrative classification with animals and objects. La Chatte in particular is also literally silenced by the whim of a white male child. Both strategies render the black presence mute. In Chopin's "A No Account Creole" blacks are generalized as "darkies" (90) and equated with animals when the narrator says, "for the little darkies had scampered away to their cabins, the dogs had run to their kennels, and the hens were puffing big with wretchedness under the scanty shelter of a fallen wagon-body" (91). The narrative is socially constructed; therefore, by nature it is subjective. The language also contradicts Seyersted's conclusion that Chopin's views are never imposed on the reader. The writer's choice of language leaves an imprint even when it is channeled subtly through the narrative voice and tone. Literally categorizing humans with animals forces the close reader to raise questions about the author's genuine interest in the depiction of human characteristics.

In concert with the local-color parade of objects above, the narrator describes the mammy figure, La Chatte, as "a broad, black woman with ends of white wool sticking out from under her tignon" (89). La Chatte's size can be inferred from the language chosen to describe how she sat "lazily and heavily on the doorstep" (89). The description follows the norm for the stereotypical mammy even in the absence of an explicit ideal white female who plays the role of mistress. The beautiful white female, Euphrasie, however, is present. She is portrayed with thick chestnut waves in her hair, wistful light eyes, red lips, and cream-colored flesh (85-86). Again, Euphrasie is present as the contrastive ideal white female even though she is not technically cast as La Chatte's mistress.

Like Chopin's "black woman" at the door in *The Awakening*, La Chatte in "A No Account Creole" is silenced by the young white male of the household—a young white male who threatens her with a gun to fulfill his desire for a particular baked good. She tells her listener, Rose, "'I goes to de ba'el, de gun's a-p'intin'. Ef I goes to de fiah, de gun's a-p'intin'. W'en I rolls out de dough, de gun 's a-p'intin'; an' him neva say nuttin', an' me a-trim'lin' like ole Uncle Noah w'en de mis'ry strike 'im'" (90). In retrospect La Chatte acceptingly views the ordeal as mischievous behavior rather than as a battle of wills or a struggle to preserve the superior-inferior hierarchy.

Finally, animal imagery again reinforces the stereotype because La Chatte's name means "cat."

"Beyond the Bayou" (1894)

In Chopin's short story "Beyond the Bayou," La Folle breaks her self-constructed silence in order to perpetuate the stereotypical behavior of loyalty, thus confirming the superior-inferior hierarchy in the white female-black female correlation. La Folle is constrained not by obvious strategies of domination such as control, silence, or invisibility, but by an emotional self-confinement. Ironically, La Folle's confinement is due to a childhood experience which left her fearful of leaving her dwelling. In her self-confinement, La Folle actually imposes a perimeter of silence because her neighbors have moved beyond the bayou over the years. As Lydia Boren suggests, La Folle, in refusing to travel beyond the bayou, subjects herself to a geographical prison (1992, 4). With the exception of obesity, La Folle is typical of most older black women portrayed in early white female literature: "She was now a large, gaunt black woman, past thirty-five. She had more physical strength than most men, and made her patch of cotton, corn and tobacco like the best of them" (175). As in other Chopin works, La Folle, too, is compared to an animal: "She walked with long strides. Her eyes were fixed desperately before her, and she breathed heavily, as a tired ox" (178). It is the ideal white female whom she desperately attempts to reach with Chéri, the white female's wounded son. Even though the narrator provides no full portrait of Chéri's mother in "Beyond the Bayou," it is understood that she holds the position of superior white female and mother, for she is the only white female inscribed in the narrative. La Folle plays the expected role of subservient mother and woman as she overcomes her own deep-seated and long-standing fears to save the life of the white boy, Chéri, whom she loved as if he were her own son.

The Silence in *The Awakening*

In Chopin's *The Awakening* (1899), the narrative silencing strategy restricts the black female presence through descriptive namelessness and partial voicelessness as she struggles to maintain her identity through work and responsibility. Regardless of role in *The Awakening*, the black presence is again portrayed as if it were an object in a local-color description: "A little black girl sat . . ." (40); "The little negro girl who worked . . ." (51); "The quadroon had vanished" (59); and "the light-colored mulatto boy . . . admitted them" (69). Yet Chopin chooses to write that "a maid . . . offered the callers liqueur" (69), without color description, so the maid may be white. All the other characters are carefully distinguished according to hue.

In *The Awakening* the stereotypical figure, however, emerges as a descriptively nameless, partially voiceless, albeit defiant black woman who communicates her discontent when she is forbidden to do her job in a way reminiscent of Stowe's Chloe or Dinah. The most meaningful scene in *The Awakening* as it pertains to the black presence and persona occurs when Victor Lebrun prevents "a black woman" from performing her duty of welcoming Edna Pontellier, his guest. The black woman's discontent is significant because a struggle ensues between this mature black woman and a 19-year-old white boy. Chopin brings to the forefront the power relationships inherent in place—blacks are always inferior to whites in their white adoptive homes (Harris 1982, xii). The struggle on the surface appears to be a white boy reprimanding a black servant for inappropriate behavior when the black servant's behavior actually represents the indoctrination of servitude:

> It was Victor who opened the gate for her [Edna Pontellier]. A black woman, wiping her hands upon her apron, was close at his heels. Before she saw them Edna could hear them in altercation, the woman—plainly an anomaly—claiming the right to be allowed to perform her duties, one of which was to answer the bell. He [Victor] instructed the black woman to go at once and inform Madame Lebrun that Mrs. Pontellier desired to see her. The woman grumbled a refusal to do *part* of her duty when she had not been permitted to do it all, and started back to her interrupted task of weeding the garden. Whereupon Victor administered a rebuke ... the rebuke was convincing, for the woman dropped her hoe and went mumbling into the house (79 emphasis added).

The black woman enacts her stereotypical mammy/negro domestic role as one who is willing and eager to do her job and who is so firmly ensconced in her defined role that she insists that the white "master" reinforce it. Any rival meets with verbal resistance; however, because Chopin's work consists of a silencing narrative strategy, this black female character is equipped with communicative channels that are inaudible to the reader. The black female desires to talk back in order to communicate her displeasure, but she has at her disposal only partially verbal mumbling and grumbling and non-verbal body language to express her displeasure that not merely the young white boy's interference, but most importantly, the white female's presence has prevented her from doing her job.

Bell hooks speaks of having been punished for talking back. Like Alice Walker, hooks points out the silences, the voices not heard, the voices of the wounded and the oppressed (hooks 1989, 6). Hooks defines talking back more meaningfully as "back talk, speaking as an equal to an authority figure, daring to disagree, to have an opinion" (hooks 1989, 5). Toni Morrison says that the "Africanist presence is permitted speech only to reinforce the slave holder's ideology" (1992, 28). Because the black woman is descriptively nameless and partially voiceless, the text omits quoted dialogue as she struggles to fully perform the work and responsibility that form the basis of her identity. It is when the white female enters that the black female is silenced. Chopin's silencing narrative strategy softens the earlier stereotypes revealed in the works of Stowe and Hentz, where contentment is vocally proclaimed but in a usurped voice. Even though the stereotype is less blatant in Chopin's works, the portrayal of the older black woman, here as elsewhere in early white female literature, still conveys a racist view of her inferiority since her identity is indistinguishable from her work and responsibility.

Birnbaum notes that this door scene in *The Awakening* is often overlooked. She describes the servant as the nameless black woman who Victor complains is imperfectly trained. Yet the woman claims the right to be able to perform her duties (1995, 326). Birnbaum suggests that the black woman's resistance is a sign of Victor's adolescent incompetence. The servant who is permitted partial voicelessness actually emasculates Victor in front of Edna Pontellier. Birnbaum agrees that the most important point is that the black female servant in the door scene is not allowed direct speech. Her language is only mediated through indirect narration (1995, 327). This correlate to Edna Pontellier then is lacking voice, name, family, community, and history, yet she is a presence which must be planted somewhere along the periphery of the writer's artistic rendition of life in order to facilitate voice and expression of desire in the white female. According to Peggy Prenshaw, the most oppressive and damaging result of the southern white female's subservience to men is that she is silent (78). If silence is imposed even on the white female, then a silencing narrative strategy that renders the black female invisible is yet another form of embellishment or excess that one must continually construct in order to maintain a position of dominance and superiority at any level, at any cost. Invisibility, then, is an embellished silence—silence in excess.

This glance at the portrayal of the mammy figure in the works of early white women writers reveals that embellished and exaggerated physical features are secondary to the portrayal of behavior consistent with the ideology of the dominant culture. Stereotypical images that perpetuate and confirm role expectations make a greater impact than physical features in confirming assumptions. Perpetuation of stereotypical images gives the dominant culture a false sense of reassurance that blacks will emulate the roles that are portrayed in order to reap the benefits that surround the stereotypical figure depicted in the literature. Through the lens of the white female cultural perspective Aunt Chloe, in Stowe's *Uncle Tom's Cabin*, conveys a sense of permanence, as if the domestic rituals over which she presides have gone on for ages and will continue into the indefinite future (Donovan 53). Although Caroline Hentz clearly conveys proslavery sentiment in *The Planter's Northern Bride* and Stowe anti-slavery sentiment in *Uncle Tom's Cabin*, character portrayal of the black female leaves the imprint that equality is neither a consideration nor a goal for either early white woman writer. Even though religion is an obvious motif in Stowe's *Uncle Tom's Cabin,* the notions of patriarchy and hierarchy are not displaced by the sentimental form in which this book was written. Chopin, too, strives for no real social change for the black woman because the silencing narrative strategy in her short stories and novel carries with it a force that parallels domination and control and perpetuates the hierarchical notion of superior-inferior.

In the literary works of early white women, finally, the ideal white female figure is linked to her correlate, the stereotypical mammy, through stereotypically defined role expectations which are created when one group dominates another, and which result in forms of work and responsibility and thus forms of identity for both the stereotypical older black woman and the ideal white female.

In the literary works of early black women writers many of the roles that the older black female assumes resemble those of the stereotypical mammy; however, in the context of, not the ideal white female, but the mulatta heroine, the significance of her roles change.

CHAPTER 3

Rhetoric of Freedom
Incidents in the Life of a Slave Girl Written by Herself

The expected characteristics of the familiar mammy figure and her roles associated with work and responsibility in the context of the ideal white female undergo a shift when we turn to the works of early black female writers. Images now emanate from the perspective of the black female. Aspects of subservience still surround the older black woman, but in many instances these aspects are associated with roles of resistance rather than complicity. In the works of early black women writers, the older black woman emerges as the foremother figure. The construction of the foremother figure is a symbol of resistance in her subversion of the stereotypical mammy image. The position of the foremother, now in the context of the mulatta heroine, reveals a figure of empowerment. The strength of her ability to subvert is thus magnified. Whether the foremother is ideal or flawed, whether she is physically free or enslaved, her powerful language frames the foremother-mulatta relationship in the works of early black female writers.

In Harriet Jacobs's *Incidents in the Life of a Slave Girl Written by Herself* (1861), Aunt Marthy plays the role of grandmother and significant older black woman and Aunt Nancy, the foremother figure in the life of the author and protagonist. Within the construction of this significant work, I will use the language again to identify and examine the roles of Aunt Marthy and Aunt Nancy in light of their life experiences, discuss their influence in Jacobs's life, and determine Jacobs's responses to their influence. Although Aunt Marthy plays a much larger role in the story of Jacobs's escape and in many ways seems to be the vocal and nurturing older woman, it is the peripheral and nearly silent Aunt Nancy whose values represent more clearly those of the ideal foremother construction and who is "clothed in her right mind."

For the first time, this study turns from fiction to a slave narrative, a form of autobiography. This work reflects the fullest dramatization of the mulatta heroine because it occurs in the first-person narrative style and is highly reflective. Jacobs tells her personal story through the thin disguise of protagonist Linda Brent. She presents her case as an individual and as a spokesperson for black females still enslaved. According to Phillipa Kafka, Jacobs also exercises caution against violating the sensibilities of her targeted white female audience when she tells her story in the form of non-threatening sentimental discourse (1993, 116-17).

Like other early black women writers, Jacobs makes choices with language use in character portrayal. It is actually out of the medium of language that the foremother figure emerges in early black women's fiction. Gwin describes Jacobs's work as a controlled creation, a creation used to control and dominate, through the medium of language, those individuals who controlled and dominated her life during her enslavement (1985a, 65). Not only those who control her life, but those who simply influence her life participate in Jacobs's controlled creation. As Jacobs creates, she revises the conventions of the sentimental novel. She defies the understandings of sexual morality and challenges readers to think about the complexity of morality and virtue. Essentially, through the telling of her story, Jacobs creates a self consistent with her experiences as a black woman. Her work demands revision of nineteenth-century women's social and literary stereotypes as well as stereotypes of the black woman—revision of the image of true womanhood (Doriani 1991, 207; Carby 1987, 61; Yellin 1985, 273).

Once again, it is clear that the images of black and white women differ in the works of early black and white female writers. Early black women writers portray the older black woman as a revision of the stereotypical mammy portrayed in early white female works. Early black women writers also yield vivid detailed descriptions of the white females in their works, including slave narratives such as Jacobs's. Many white female writers, however, depict black women in stereotypical modes in fictional and nonfictional works. They seem not to have known black women as individuals. Chapter Two of this study notes, and Gwin also concludes, that blacks were of importance to many white females only in terms of their abilities to render services and to reflect white images—to act as a correlate for the white female. Individual characteristics were important if they represented the presence or absence of the threats of disloyalty or sexual competition (1985a, 97). Reflecting on this early black and white female relationship at its worst, Jacobs says of Mrs. Flint, "She pitied herself as a martyr, but she was incapable of feeling for the condition of shame and misery in which her unfortunate, helpless slave was placed" (Yellin 1987, 33). Jacobs observes also that Mrs. Flint recognizes no family ties among blacks. Mrs. Flint expects Aunt Nancy, her housekeeper, to be buried in her family plot, a cemetery exclusive to whites. She wants Aunt Nancy to remain at her feet in death as she did in life. It is only after the doctor brings to Mrs. Flint's attention the likelihood that Aunt Nancy's family might wish to have some say in Aunt Nancy's burial (146) that Mrs. Flint realizes the limits of her possessiveness of what she perceives to be her property and a mainstay in her life. Viguerie claims that the white female sees the mammy as an integral member of the white family and can thus easily love her. Such inclusion, of course, implies exclusion from the black family and thus the black community (1993, 107).

The ambivalent nature of some of the white and black female relationships is apparent in the relationship between Mrs. Flint and Aunt Nancy. For example, Mrs. Flint permits Aunt Nancy to marry yet insists that she sleep on the floor as usual outside her chamber, even on her wedding night (143). Ambivalence is also apparent when Aunt Nancy is placed in jail in an effort to bring her niece, Jacobs (Linda), out of hiding during her attempted escape, yet Aunt Nancy is later released at Mrs. Flint's request. In the context of her white mistress, Aunt Nancy is thus portrayed here as the mammy figure. Both Christian and Faust confirm that the presence of the mammy is necessary in order to maintain the image of the ideal white female under a patriarchal system. Jacobs explicitly undermines the stereotype, however, when she mockingly explains that "My aunt was taken out of jail at the end of a month, because Mrs. Flint could not spare her any longer. She was tired of being her own housekeeper. It was quite too fatiguing to order her dinner and eat it too" (101). Still another example of the ambivalent nature of the relationship between the black and white female occurs when:

> Aunt Nancy one night asked permission to watch with her sick
> mother, and Mrs. Flint replied, 'I don't see any need of your going. I
> can't spare you.' But when she found other ladies in the
> neighborhood were so attentive, not wishing to be outdone in
> Christian charity, she . . . stood by the bedside of her [Aunt Marthy]
> who had loved her in her infancy, and who had been repaid by such
> grievous wrongs (123-24).

According to Gwin, the white female's ambivalence toward the black
female and her inability to acknowledge her humanity may be
approached as a paradigm for this paradoxical pattern of connection
and rejection in the southern racial experience, an experience that is
mirrored in the literature (1985, 109).

Race intermingling in the context of white and black female
relations and in the context of white male and black female relations is
inscribed in the text since the language of literature is sensitive to the
social concerns of the period. Aunt Marthy, for example, was the
daughter of a white southern planter. She has borne five children, one
of whom is Linda's mother; however, the text tells the reader nothing
about Aunt Marthy's husband or the father of her children. The only
implicit reference to Aunt Marthy's husband and Jacobs's grandfather
is that among Marthy's five children, Benjamin "inherited the
complexion my grandmother had derived from Anglo-Saxon ancestors"
(6). Since Benjamin inherited his fair complexion from his
grandmother, then Benjamin's father must have presented the
possibility of a competing darker complexion. Because there is no full
reference to color, the reader can presume that Jacobs's maternal
grandfather is black; thus her mother is a quadroon and Jacobs an
octoroon. Jacobs, however, describes both her mother and father as
mulattoes (5). She substantiates the mixed race of her father when she
tells much later in her story that her paternal grandfather is white (78).
For the sake of consistency and to convey that the heroine is of the
mixed black and white races, I will simply refer to Jacobs (Linda) as
the mulatta heroine.

Jacobs mixes praise and admiration in the inscription of her
grandmother, a significant figure in this work. Aunt Marthy is an
entrepreneur who is well-loved in the community by both blacks and
whites (6). She is mistress of a "snug little home" surrounded by the
necessities of life. Jacobs sees her grandmother as loving, sympathetic,
patient, and hopeful. She takes the time to listen to Linda and her

brother (17). Aunt Marthy is like a balm, something that has the power to soothe, to satisfy, and to heal. It is when Jacobs's senses are activated and she smells, tastes, hears, and touches within the confines of her grandmother's home that her grandmother's words generate hope and contentment: "We longed for a home like hers. There was always found sweet balsam for our troubles. . . . There was a grand big oven there, too, that baked bread and nice things from town" (17). Outside the context of this nurturing environment, however, contentment is elusive. It is the home, the domestic ideal, that makes everything seem so right, so hopeful when Jacobs is in the presence of this wise older black woman whose life experiences reflect that she was freed, re-enslaved, and eventually freed again.

Aunt Marthy not only participated in, but orchestrated the final action that marked her freedom. As Linda would do later, Aunt Marthy takes control of her situation—a situation constructed by the vindictive Dr. Flint. What Dr. Flint desired to do in private, Aunt Marthy made public:

> When the day of sale came, she took her place among the chattels, and at the first call she sprang upon the auction-block. Many voices called out, 'Shame! Shame! Who is going to sell you, Aunt Marthy? Don't stand there! That is no place for you' (11).

No one out-bids her dead mistress' sister, who purchases her for $50.00 and releases her immediately from the bondage of slavery (12). Martha Cutter points out that this passage represents discourse which is both communal and performative (1996, 221). The community and Miss Fannie, her dead mistress' sister, erect a strategic language front that overrides Dr. Flint's maneuvers. Through discourse, Aunt Marthy and the community combine forces to make a public shame out of what Dr. Flint wished to do quickly and privately. This action reconfigures a dreaded component of slavery, the auction block, the life force of the system of slavery. The auction block is a stark reminder that slaves were viewed as objects. It reduces every Negro (whether mentally enslaved or mentally free) to the lowest common factors of merchandise, property, and economic profit and loss. The auction block extinguishes the spirit of the slave because it disrupts families and creates fear, anxiety, and madness all for the sake of someone else's economic gain. Aunt Marthy, then, took action that resulted not only in her individual freedom but in the maintenance of her family unit. She was proactive, not reactive, in her counter-move to Dr. Flint's decision to sell her. Aunt Marthy serves as a model for what Jacobs would do later in that she plans and participates in an action that steals the reins of power from Dr. Flint's hands. Likewise, Jacobs steals the reins of power from Dr. Flint's hands when she submits to another white male's pressure for sexual relations, bears two children by this white male, imprisons herself in a garret for seven years, and eventually escapes the bondage of slavery. It has been said repeatedly that where there is no slave there can be no master. Aunt Marthy serves as an earlier and Jacobs as a later model for this maxim.

The modeling influence of Aunt Marthy's language is evident when Jacobs attempts to comfort her brother William after their father's mysterious death: "perhaps we might before long be allowed to hire our time, and then we could earn money to buy our freedom" (10). These words parallel the actions of Aunt Marthy, who used her midnight baking as a means to save money and purchase the freedom of her children (6). The strengthening influence of Aunt Marthy also emerges in Jacobs's discourse when she parallels Aunt Marthy's disdain for Dr. Flint: "My grandmother had already had high words with my master about me. She had told him pretty plainly what she thought of his character" (53). In response to Dr. Flint's accusations following the revelation of her pregnancy ("He talked of . . . how I had sinned against my master. . . ."), Jacobs replies forcefully, as she has repeatedly done utilizing the discourses of resistance, sass and back-talk, "I have sinned against God and myself, but not against you" (58). The strengthening influence of Aunt Marthy is explicitly and lovingly summarized in Jacobs's language when she says that she is "indebted to her for all my comforts, spiritual or temporal" (11).

Aunt Marthy is a model of strength and support, but her perspective, intertwined with a mother's possessive love, is problematic. She is strong and honest, and demands respect, but her language reveals that her perspective is impaired by the system of slavery when she envisions freedom for her children and grandchildren. For example, when her youngest son, Benjamin, is captured after his attempted escape, Aunt Marthy tells him to "Put your trust in God." Benjamin responds that "When a man is hunted like a wild beast he forgets there is a God, a heaven." Aunt Marthy pleads, "Be humble, my child, and your master [owner] will forgive you." Benjamin responds with conviction: "No! I will never humble myself to him." Benjamin confirms the attributes of his mother's character in his calmer response to her, "I wish I had some of your goodness. You bear every thing patiently, just as though you thought it was all right." Yet Aunt Marthy, understanding her son, reveals a facet of her own earlier character when she admits that in her younger years, like Benjamin, she did not rely on God for guidance (22).

Aunt Marthy can be credited for influencing the lives of her son Benjamin, her daughter Aunt Nancy, and her granddaughter Jacobs, because her actions are always an attempt to preserve the family, not her individual self. She represents the communal and the collective as opposed to the individual. Aunt Marthy labors for the freedom of her family, and in doing so she clings to the belief that freedom can be bought and that one must pay into the system in order to be free of the system. Her son and daughter, Benjamin and Aunt Nancy, possess a consciousness of liberation, however, that reflects that they know freedom is their birthright and that the system of slavery is merely a deterrent. Benjamin will leave all for freedom, while Aunt Nancy will persist in her revolutionary stance of "freedom now." Aunt Marthy will remain with her children in virtual enslavement until her death, or until all of her children are free.

Aunt Marthy reveals again that her perspective is impaired by the system of slavery when she condemns Jacobs for her pregnancy. Upon hearing Mrs. Flint's accusation concerning Jacobs's pregnancy, Aunt Marthy says to her granddaughter, "'O Linda! has it come to this? I had rather see you dead than to see you as you now are. You are a disgrace to your dead mother'" (56). Surely Aunt Marthy would not take the word of the white mistress who verbally abuses her granddaughter and physically abuses her own daughter, Aunt Nancy. In her motherly wisdom, Aunt Marthy must have suspected Jacobs's predicament because the community knew by Jacobs's countenance and her maturity what she was experiencing in the Flint household: "They all knew well the guilty practices under that roof; and they were aware that to speak of them was an offence that never went unpunished" (28).

Even though *Incidents in the Life of a Slave Girl* mourns the violation of black womanhood, maternity, family, and home (Tate 1992, 26), Jacobs's response to sexual oppression reflects her unwillingness to succumb to powerlessness and passivity (Doriani 1991, 209). Thus Jacobs identifies the white Mr. Sands, not Dr. Flint, as the father of her child. Even though Aunt Marthy's judgment of Linda is in line with the Victorian views of the time and the system of slavery, Jacobs questions the adequacy of this judgment and reaches toward an alternative moral code (Yellin 1985, 270-272). Jacobs's plea to her audience is also a plea to her grandmother and those who possess the strict moral attitude of her grandmother. She makes the claim that the female slave does not live under the same conditions as the white female and thus believes "that the slave woman ought not to be judged by the same standard as others" (56). Jacobs challenges the sexual ideology of the white world and holds a more complex standard of morality. She attaches value to the act of willingly submitting to a lover (Doriani 1991, 210) outside the boundaries of marriage and race. Jacobs can value such an act comparatively as she devalues the act by which the threatening master dominates the unwilling slave through rape. Such a presumption is projected as incredible for the white female reader, who does not possess the capability to truly see and thus to know this black female, who exists in every aspect of her life.

Claudia Tate observes that when Mr. Sands appears in the text, the text switches conventions from those of sentimental fiction to those of the novel of seduction in order to re-inscribe the prescribed sexual character of the heroine from innocence to experience. According to Tate, Jacobs's playing the role of the seductress instead of the seduced victim is radical and revolutionary for a woman to record, whether slave or free, black or white (1992, 109). It is understandable that Tate describes Jacobs as a "seductress" because the word connotes agency, whereas the word "seduced" connotes passivity. Following Jacobs's lead, Tate attributes a sense of power to the fact that she chooses to yield to one white male over another. It is only figuratively, however, that Jacobs wields some form of power. Jacobs could not initially tell her grandmother the history that preceded her deliberately calculated move to submit to Mr. Sands. She could not talk to her grandmother intimately about her personal shame (57), because "I feared her as well as loved her. I had been accustomed to look up to her with a respect bordering upon awe" (28-29).

Although Aunt Marthy is highly respected among friends and family members, her strong views on the act of escaping to freedom stand in direct opposition to the views of the black community: "She was strongly opposed to her children's undertaking any such project" (42). With escape comes the danger of capture and torture. Aunt Marthy wishes to protect her children, so she cries in anguish when her grandson William escapes from Mr. Sands and remains in the North. Aunt Marthy is obviously the exception to the rule in the black community, for even her neighbor, Aunt Aggie, is puzzled over her sadness, since sadness and freedom are mutually exclusive. She urges Aunt Marthy to rejoice in her grandson's escape to freedom:

> 'Git down on your knees and bress de Lord! I don't know whar my poor chillern is, and I nebber 'spect to know. You don't know whar poor Linda's gone to; but you do know whar her brudder is. He is in free parts; and dat's de right place' (135).

Aunt Marthy still communicates deterrence when she speaks directly to Jacobs about her anticipated escape: "Stand by your own children, and suffer with them till death" (91). Aunt Marthy does not realize that Jacobs, like her brother William and her Aunt Nancy, possesses a different world view and thus a different view of freedom. Still, Aunt Marthy attempts a further cruelly indirect approach to deter Linda when she says to Linda's children, "'Poor little souls! what would you do without a mother? She don't love you as I do'" (91). For Aunt Marthy a mother's love is a sacrificial love. To love means to remain with the children regardless. Responsible motherhood, then, is sacrificial.

Despite all the drawbacks associated with Aunt Marthy's character, she still clearly represents a refutation of the stereotypical mammy figure as shown in her defiance of Dr. Flint and the priority she attaches to her own family. Jacobs challenges the stereotypical, the conventional, and the ideological. Jacobs's portrayal, not only of Aunt Marthy but of other slave women, contradicts the image of slave women as subservient victims. For example, Betty's voice emerges in a portrait which seemingly resembles the mammy figure in white female literature. Her mistress describes her as "so faithful that I would trust my own life with her" (99). Betty's voice, however, emerges not to praise her mistress, but to console Jacobs while she is temporarily sheltered in the home of the sympathetic white benefactress and her children are in jail. Betty consoles Linda with tough love by saying, "'Lors, chile! what's you crying 'bout? Dem young uns vil kill you dead. Don't be so chick'n hearted! If you does, you vil nebber git thro' dis world'" (101). Even though Betty has no children, she possesses the cultural attributes of mothering and mother wit when she diagnoses Jacobs's condition, assesses the situation, and takes action: "'You's got de highsterics. I'll sleep wid you to-night. . . . Something has stirred you up mightily. When you done cryin, I'll talk wid you'" (108). Ironically, both Betty and Aunt Nancy are childless, yet they exemplify the cultural aspect of community in the concept of the extended family.

Betty and Aunt Nancy communicate freedom, regardless of the ties that bind. Jacobs, then, associates cultural attitudes and attributes with the older black women who make up her community, especially with Aunt Nancy. Although both Aunt Marthy and Aunt Nancy possess characteristics of the foremother figure as they play the role of distinguishing the mulatta heroine, it is Aunt Nancy who, though emerging in fewer speech situations, makes the greater impact on Jacobs's life.

It is ironic that Aunt Marthy, who is free, is not liberated, and Aunt Nancy, who is enslaved, is liberated and clothed in her right mind. Aunt Nancy possesses a consciousness of liberation and speaks liberation even though she is physically and spatially bound. Alice Walker separates this intuitive knowledge from textbook knowledge when she captures the sense of knowing that Aunt Nancy possesses. Walker refers to those foremothers who "knew what we must know without knowing a page of it themselves" (1983b, 242-43). Aunt Nancy has not experienced freedom, but she embraces freedom and wants for Jacobs and her children in life what she will experience only in death— freedom from enslavement. Freedom is something she wants so much that Jacobs's experiencing it will serve vicariously for Aunt Nancy. Aunt Nancy transforms everything she does to work toward the liberation of Jacobs and her children. She even suffers in jail with other family members, to Jacobs's dismay: "But it added to my pain, to think that the good old aunt, who had always been so kind to her sister's orphan children, should be shut up in prison for no other crime than loving them" (101). Aunt Nancy never complains when she participates in Jacobs's movement toward freedom, even taking risks to obtain information for Jacobs. She serves as a reporter when she obtains information in the Flint household and communicates that information to Jacobs during her self-imprisonment in the garret. She realizes fully the significance of this information to Jacobs's safety and plans for her eventual and successful escape.

Although Jacobs shares her own experiences in the Flint household with the reading audience, she does not share the experiences of Aunt Nancy, who lives in the same household for years as a housekeeper and waiting maid. Jacobs also does not tell the reader about Aunt Nancy's physical features. Again, Aunt Nancy's younger brother, Benjamin, must serve as the basis for a sketch of a textual portrait: "He was a bright handsome lad, nearly white; for he inherited the complexion my grandmother had derived from Anglo-Saxon ancestors" (6). Also when the slave trader purchases Benjamin following his imprisonment, "He said he would give any price if the handsome lad was a girl" (23). The reader can deduce that Aunt Nancy was an attractive black woman and thus a potential victim under the control of the obsessive Dr. Flint. Did Jacobs suppress her knowledge of Dr. Flint's sexual abuse of Aunt Nancy to protect the name of her dearly beloved aunt? Jacobs admits in the Preface of *Incidents in the Life of a Slave Girl* that "I have not exaggerated the wrongs inflicted by Slavery; on the contrary, my descriptions fall far short of the facts. . . . I had no motive for secrecy on my own account, but I deemed it kind and considerate towards others to pursue this course" (1). The title of Jacobs's work informs the reader, too, that her work is limited to the revelation of the incidents in *her* life, not the incidents in the lives of Aunt Marthy and Aunt Nancy.

Jacobs reserves Chapter 28 for Aunt Nancy, but the chapter still does not render the complexity of her person. Claudia Tate says that Aunt Nancy serves as the epilogue to Aunt Marthy's story. She is Linda's ideal surrogate mother because she is her real mother's twin sister. Her niece is the only way Aunt Nancy can experience motherhood after the deaths of all eight of her premature babies (1992, 110). I disagree with Tate's assessment that Aunt Nancy serves as an epilogue to Aunt Marthy's story, for Aunt Nancy's inscription as the foremother figure counters the notion that she is of lesser importance. That she is a minor character and therefore not prominent in the text is a general characteristic of the foremother figure. Jacobs's personal view of Aunt Nancy is that "she was a kind, good aunt to me; . . . She was, in fact, at the beginning and end of every thing" (12). In the Flint household she is the housekeeper, waiting maid, and nurse: "nothing went on well without her" (144). Jacobs also says that her Aunt Nancy is "old" during the time that she slept with her while she lived in the Flint household: "At night I slept by the side of my great [sic] aunt, where I felt safe. He was too prudent to come into her room. She was an old woman, and had been in the family many years" (32-33). Aunt Nancy must, however, be roughly the same age as her mistress, Mrs. Flint, because Aunt Marthy was forced to wean her own baby (Aunt Nancy's twin sister and Linda's mother) early so as to accommodate the needs of the baby that would mature to be Mrs. Flint (7). At the age of 15, Linda comments that Dr. Flint is 40 years her senior; thus he is approximately 55 years old (27). Mrs. Flint is his second wife and his junior (34); thus Aunt Nancy, even though Linda describes her as "old," is some years younger than Dr. Flint.

What all this leads to is the likelihood that Dr. Flint attempted to victimize Aunt Nancy over the years as he did Linda. This suspicion arises not only because of the evidence of her younger age and physical beauty, implied in the text, but because of the number of babies she bore prematurely. Jacobs says that Aunt Nancy married a seafaring man at the age of 20 (143), so her husband was thus seldom at home. Even though she was married, Mrs. Flint insisted that Aunt Nancy sleep on the floor outside her chamber: "But on the wedding evening, the bride was ordered to her old post on the entry floor" (143). This ongoing involuntary separation from her husband leads one to question how Aunt Nancy became pregnant six times and lost six babies before she was permitted to sleep in her own quarters. Even after moving into her own quarters to sleep, Aunt Nancy becomes pregnant two more times and both babies die. Jacobs, like others in the community, knew Dr. Flint to be the father of eleven children of slaves (35). Jacobs refers to the way in which Dr. Flint removed those slaves who publicly acknowledged his paternity because it was a crime for a slave mother to identify the white father of her child (13).

These textual implications of Aunt Nancy's experiences in the Flint household also strengthen my argument about the close and meaningful relationship between Aunt Nancy and Jacobs. Theirs is familial and experiential in nature, as is evident in the foremother's limited, repetitive, and powerful messages to the mulatta heroine and the mulatta heroine's limited, meaningful, and responsive references to the foremother. It is also configured on textual implications and absence. Omission and absence are meaningful in language use.

In contrast to Aunt Marthy, not once do we hear Aunt Nancy condemn Jacobs while she maneuvers through the mire of enslavement and oppression. Aunt Nancy communicates one clear message— freedom now. This enslaved older black woman who possesses a consciousness of liberation, as her brother Benjamin does, is referred to only intermittently in the text and does not have the privilege of direct language use at the same level as her mother, Aunt Marthy. Aunt Nancy is, however, permitted voice when she communicates the message of freedom to Jacobs during her self-imprisonment in the garret: "'I am old, and have not long to live . . . and I could die happy if I could only see you and the children free'" (144). Aunt Nancy communicates the urgency of freedom, for she sees the systemic perpetuation of enslavement when she gazes upon Jacobs and her children. Whereas Aunt Marthy's language discourages escape, Aunt

Nancy's language encourages escape—freedom by any means. Jacobs recalls her Aunt's powerful message: "She said if I persevered I might, perhaps, gain the freedom of my children; and *even if I perished* in doing it, that was better than to leave them to groan under the same persecutions that had blighted my own life" (144 emphasis added). The foremother's language in this example, even though reported indirectly, has made a deep impact on the mulatta heroine, reinforcing her determination to escape.

Aunt Nancy's language reveals the power of characterization. Gwin credits Jacobs with using the language as a controlled creation, while McDowell discusses characterization and authentic representation of speech in general. McDowell says that one of the most challenging aspects of characterization for any writer is the authentic representation of speech and consideration for the relationship between author and audience. This relationship determines and explains not just narrative voice, but a range of artistic strategies and choices (1987, 283). The character Aunt Nancy conveys a message to Jacobs's audience through brevity, clarity, and repetition. Through language this foremother conveys an attitude, a perspective, and a determination that is unshakable. There is simply no substitute for freedom. Even though Aunt Nancy's voice is minimal, the family relies on her judgment and is guided by her advice (144). Clearly Jacobs is guided by Aunt Nancy's advice when she recalls, "When my friends tried to discourage me from running away, she always encouraged me. . . . she sent me word never to yield" (144). Of Aunt Marthy Jacobs recalls, "Most earnestly did she strive to make us feel that it was the will of God; that He had seen fit to place us under such circumstances; and though it seemed hard, we ought to pray for contentment" (17). It is because of Aunt Marthy that Phillip refuses to seize the opportunity for freedom when, on an errand, he meets his brother Benjamin in New York shortly after Benjamin's escape. Aunt Marthy's influence motivates Phillip to forego freedom and return home. Phillip tells his younger brother Benjamin that "it would kill their mother if he deserted her in her trouble" (25). Jacobs confesses just prior to her attempted escape that Aunt Marthy influences her thoughts and actions: "My courage failed me, in view of the sorrow I should bring on that faithful, loving old heart" (91). Aunt Marthy's language inhibits her; Aunt Nancy's language empowers her.

Not only is the foremother-mulatta heroine relationship based on familial ties and suspected abuse, but Aunt Nancy and Jacobs share similarly traumatic physical experiences. Jacobs describes the circumstances surrounding her first birth: "When my babe was born, they said it was premature. It weighed only four pounds; but God let it live. I heard the doctor say I could not survive till morning. . . . but now I could not die" (60-61). Aunt Nancy is described as having "given premature birth to six children; and all the while she was employed as night-nurse to Mrs. Flint's children. . . . toiling all day and being deprived of her rest at night" (143). After eight births and eight deaths Aunt Nancy resolved, "it is not the will of God that any of my children should live" (144). During Jacobs's self-imprisonment, she suffers inadequate physical mobility in the garret and over-exposure to the weather: "My limbs were benumbed by inaction, and the cold filled them with cramp. I had a very painful sensation of coldness in my head; even my face and tongue stiffened, and I lost the power of speech" (122). Of Aunt Nancy, who suffered the physical hardship of sleeping on the floor for years, she says: "My aunt had been stricken with paralysis. She lived but two days, and the last day she was speechless" (144-45). Not only is the relationship between Aunt Nancy and Jacobs illuminated here, but the close relationship between Aunt Marthy and Aunt Nancy is evident especially during Aunt Nancy's final days of life:

> She [Aunt Marthy] was grateful for permission to watch by the death-bed of her child. They had always been devoted to each other; and now they sat looking into each other's eyes, longing to speak of the secret that had weighed so much on the hearts of both. . . . Even the hard-hearted doctor was a little softened when he saw the dying woman try to smile on the aged mother, who was kneeling by her side (144-45).

The scene makes a significant impact on Jacobs. Upon overhearing her Uncle Phillip tell someone else, "She is dead," Jacobs faints and then awakens with a fixed gaze (145). Phillip's pronouncement of death is generative; in the power of the word, death is life for Jacobs, and death is freedom for Jacobs and Aunt Nancy. Thus from an African cultural perspective Phillip enacts *nommo*, the generative power of the word, for the spirit of Aunt Nancy, now Jacobs's ancestor, binds with Jacobs's spirit and quickens her seven-year dormancy. It is only after Jacobs hears of Aunt Nancy's death that she finds the courage to escape from her seven-year self-imprisonment, and from enslavement to freedom.

Aunt Nancy, "who had been my refuge during the shameful persecutions I suffered from him [Dr. Flint]" (143), symbolically continues to serve as a refuge for Jacobs. Just as the foremother sheltered Jacobs physically within the confines of the Flint household, so she shelters her spiritually in her progress toward freedom.

In conclusion, Aunt Marthy, who is prominent in the text, is like a mother figure to Jacobs because she protects, sacrifices, advises, and loves within the boundaries prescribed by the institution of slavery. Aunt Marthy longs for freedom for her children and grandchildren, but she is willing to work her way out of an oppressive system according to the rules and laws of the oppressor. She also judges her grandchild according to Christian standards of purity derived from the white slave owners. Her words and actions communicate ambivalence. The true foremother, Aunt Nancy, on the other hand, is not prominent in the text in terms of the space permitted for her language and the language of others regarding her. To increase Aunt Nancy's presence in the text would likely have resulted in revelations about her marital relationship and her personal experiences in the Flint household. Although Aunt Nancy in her role as foremother is permitted little space for language use, her message of freedom for Jacobs and her children is clear: "'I shan't mind being a slave all my life, if I can only see you and the children free'" (129). Aunt Nancy's message is clear, concise, and repetitive giving her voice a greater force than Aunt Marthy's. Freedom requires no deliberation, negotiation, or transaction; it is to be attained by any means. In response to Aunt Nancy's repeated message, Jacobs releases herself from her seven-year self-imprisonment in the garret, escapes to the North, struggles to maintain her freedom, and works to support the livelihood and education of her children.

CHAPTER 4

Grandmothers, Mothers, and Acquaintances
The Novels of Frances E. W. Harper

Freedom and education are motifs in each of Frances Harper's works, literally and figuratively. Harper's works center on women and the significant role they play in the home, community, and society. It is useful, therefore, to determine how the foremother-mulatta heroine relationship, coupled with the motifs of freedom and education, affects the home, community, and society of blacks in Harper's four novels. Three of these are rediscovered novels of which parts of the manuscripts were missing at the time of publication: *Minnie's Sacrifice* (1869), *Sowing and Reaping: A Temperance Story* (1876-77), and *Trial and Triumph* (1888-89). The fourth is her well-known last novel *Iola Leroy or Shadows Uplifted* (1892). A stark contrast between Harper's last novel and her earlier novels lies in characterization. Harper's last novel *Iola Leroy* inscribes color, physical, and language variations in characterization. Few such variations occur in *Minnie's Sacrifice* and *Trial and Triumph*, and no variations exist in *Sowing and Reaping*.

Like Harper in *Sowing and Reaping* a number of other black women writers chose not to focus on race in their works published during the 1890s. Writers such as Amelia E. Johnson, Emma Dunham Kelley, and Katherine Davis Chapman Tillman chose not to use racially marked characters or racial themes. Admittedly it is difficult to argue in support of a foremother-mulatta heroine relationship in this study when neither character is defined in part according to racially distinct physical and behavioral characteristics. For example, Emma Dunham

Kelley's *Megda* (1891) inscribes the wisdom of the foremother in the combined foremother persona of Megda's mother and sister, Mrs. Randal and Elsie Randal respectively, but with no reference to race. Similarly, Amelia E. Johnson's Aunt Sarah Martin in *The Hazeley Family* (1894) emerges as a semblance of the foremother figure because this strict, no-nonsense, childless widow takes action and uses language that result in a sustained positive influence in the life of her niece, Flora. Amelia Johnson's *Clarence and Corinne* inscribes a foremother-like character whose language influences Clarence Burton directly and Corinne Burton indirectly within a text which, however, uses no color variation. On the other hand, Katherine Davis Chapman Tillman selects a title that emphasizes race in *Beryl Weston's Ambition: The Story of an Afro-American Girl's Life* (1893). Yet Tillman inscribes the figure of Binie within the contexts of physical disability and artistic talent with little emphasis on color and behavioral variation that can be associated with the foremother figure found in other works. These writers are often referred to as minor black women writers because they published few works and few publications regarding their works are available. In general, these "raceless" texts, like Harper's *Sowing and Reaping*, are not among the texts chosen for this study because it is difficult to establish a definitive foremother-mulatta relationship based on character portrayal and language use. Like *Sowing and Reaping,* Harper's earlier novels serialized in the *Christian Recorder*, the journal of the African Methodist Episcopal Church (1994, xi), assume a Negro reading audience; thus Negro characterization may be implied even in seemingly raceless novels. It is readily apparent, however, in Harper's *Minnie's Sacrifice* and *Trial and Triumph*, which subvert the mammy stereotype with foremother figures.

MRS. HESTON AND MIRIAM IN *MINNIE'S SACRIFICE*

Mrs. Heston in *Minnie's Sacrifice* (1869) has experienced societal ills first hand and emerges as the foremother figure who makes the greatest impact on the life of the mulatta heroine, Minnie. Mrs. Heston shares her experiences with others while visiting in the home of the sympathetic Mr. & Mrs. Hickman; thus her language becomes an educational resource for her audience (46). Her story is not filtered through someone else's opinionated view of her circumstances; she speaks as a witness, and therefore the impact on the listener is greater.

Minnie, one of Mrs. Heston's listeners, views her story as both interesting and dreadful. She hears about the inequality in travel accommodations, the denial of access to many public places and events, the denial of basic education, and discrimination in employment practices. It is the events, the details, and the pauses along with the repetitions and the intonations that result in a quality of expressiveness that moves the listener.

Paule Marshall states that blacks possess an expressive quality, a strength that comes from suffering (40). In addition to this expressive quality, the very act of telling is generative in that performance becomes interactive—the generative power of reciprocity develops between speaker and listener as the speaker relives the experiences and the listener experiences the story. Mrs. Heston's story brings Minnie to a new level of awareness, where she now has a better understanding of the wickedness and cruelty of prejudice. Minnie, who thinks herself to be white, later expresses her anguish, "'Oh, father, . . . how wicked and cruel this prejudice. Oh, how I should hate to be colored!'" (48). Prior to Minnie's hearing Mrs. Heston's story, the text indicates only that she is aware of Louis Le Croix's pro-slavery views, but her opinions and thoughts are not revealed. Apparently being in the company of a pro-slavery young man did not greatly disturb Minnie because when her father asked how she liked him, she responded, "'Oh, I was much pleased with him. We had a very pleasant time together'" (44). The missing text of chapter 10 may provide more information to clarify Minnie's former attitude prior to hearing Mrs. Heston's story. Yet judging from her adopted parents' "exchanged mournful glances" (48) in response to Minnie's expressed anguish about the wickedness of slavery, it is doubtful that she held any strong opinion about race and prejudice prior to hearing Mrs. Heston's story.

Because Minnie's level of awareness is raised after hearing Mrs. Heston's story, her mind and spirit are no longer at ease. Her thoughts are disturbed (46) and lay the groundwork for the life-transforming news that she has negro blood in her own veins. Minnie gives an initially matter-of-fact response upon hearing her adopted father's confession, "'Minnie, I believe there is a small portion of colored blood in thy veins.'" She says, "'It is enough,' drawing closer to the strange woman" (51). Still, in response to this revelation about her mixed heritage Minnie becomes "nervous and excited" and later contracts a "very high fever" followed by "a low nervous affection" (52). She confesses later to Camilla that "'at first I shrank from the social ostracism to which that knowledge doomed me, and it was some time before I was reconciled to the change'" (72). It is evident that Mrs. Heston's story is linked to Minnie's thoughts and has altered her world view when she explains to Camilla, "'Oh, there are lessons of life that we never learn in the bowers of ease. They must be learned in the fire'" (72). Minnie embraces this world view and uses it as a guiding principle when she later engages in a life of teaching and counseling the freed people who rely so little on tangible, material things and so much on intangible, spiritual things.

A final observation which links Mrs. Heston's influence to Minnie's life is Minnie's statement to Camilla:

> "So, when I found out that I was colored, I made up my mind that I would neither be pitied nor patronized by my former friends; but that I would live out my own individuality and do for my race, as a colored woman, what I never could accomplish as a white woman" (72).

Minnie's words echo Mrs. Heston's sentiment in response to Mrs. Hickman's expression of pity after hearing the chronicling of her life. Mrs. Heston says with conviction, "'it is not pity we want, it is justice'" (46). Both speak from a womanist perspective as they include the community of blacks in their envisioning of a more perfect society. Minnie plans to do for her race and Mrs. Heston speaks for the group when she uses the plural, inclusive, subject pronoun, "we."

A less important but still significant foremother figure in *Minnie's Sacrifice* is the older black female, Miriam, who, through Louis Le Croix, ultimately affects the life of the mulatta heroine, Minnie. Miriam realizes the negative impact that Louis's ignorance about his mixed heritage would have on the black community, so she decides for political and cultural reasons to inform him of his mixed heritage before he goes off to the Civil War: "Miriam took up the unfinished sentence,'—because to join the secesh is to raise your hands agin your own race.' 'My own race?' and Louis laughed scornfully. . . . What do you mean, Miriam?'" (59) Miriam speaks with authority, "like some ancient prophetess":

> "I mean that you, Louis Le Croix, white as you look, are colored, and that you are my own daughter's child, and if it had not been for Miss

Camilla, who's been such an angel to you, that you would have been
a slave to-day, and then you wouldn't have been a Confederate" (59).

Reeling from Miriam's voice of authority and operating under the
urgency of War, Louis instinctively, rather than intellectually, heeds to
Miriam's advice and travels among the enslaved in order to be free.
During his escape to the North, Louis confirms Miriam's warning to
distrust whites and trust blacks. He learns that the cohesiveness of the
black community relies on its codes of silence, acts of sacrifice,
interdependency, and trust. Because of the timing and truthfulness of
Miriam's words, Louis successfully escapes to the North and following
the War participates fully in the uplift of the black race.

Minnie is then the indirect recipient of Miriam's gift of knowledge
to Louis when she marries him and they set out to help the new
freedman together. Mrs. Heston's story of her life, coupled with the
revelation of Minnie's mixed heritage, has changed Minnie's view of
the world. Miriam's revealing Louis's mixed heritage propels him into
circumstances that change his view of the world. Minnie and Louis can
only become one in thought and one in marriage because of the new
experiences ushered into their lives through the language of Mrs.
Heston and Miriam. With similarly mixed heritages and newly formed
goals to work for their race, Louis works to build his community
politically and economically, while Minnie shares with the community
the womanly arts that she learned from her adopted mother, Anna (74).
Minnie teaches the newly freed slaves knowledge of books and
homemaking while she listens to their stories of suffering; yet Minnie
too is not fully a part of the community, for the people perceive her to
be of a higher class than they are when they express, "'She mighty
good; we's low down, but she feels for we'" (75). Class differences
inscribed and implied reflect the discourse of racial uplift promoted
during the late nineteenth century. For example, class differences are
implied by the home as an extension of the person here as elsewhere in
early white and black women's literature. Minnie and Louis's dwelling
is described as a "pleasant home" (75), while Minnie visits the "humble
homes" and "lowly cabins of these newly freed people" (75). Similar to
Louis, Minnie communicates the "us" and "them" distance in the
language when she tells her mother about the hard times of colored
people, "'How wonderful is this faith! How real it is to them! How near
some of these suffering people have drawn to God!'" (82). The basis of
this distance lies in the fact that Minnie does not share the experiences

of the Negro in her formative years. Even though she accepts her mixed heritage, she remains, like Louis, somewhat of a spectator in the life experiences of the Negro. Like Mrs. Heston's story of her experiences that transformed Minnie's life, the stories of the freed people have a strengthening impact on her life, but it is something Minnie has never experienced or will never experience: "'I often feel strengthened after visiting some of these good old souls, and getting glimpses into their inner life'" (83).

Minnie teaches the people, but during the process she learns the culture—her first lesson of which came from the foremother, Mrs. Heston. Minnie's development begins from her hearing and reacting to Mrs. Heston's story. Her strong reaction, "'Oh how I should hate to be colored'" changes from pity and dread to reflection, collaboration, and action. She reflects in the speech situation with Camilla: "'But now, when I look back upon those days of gloom and suffering, I think they were among the most fruitful of my life, for in those days of pain and sorrow my resolution was formed to join the fortunes of my mother's race'" (72). She collaborates with her husband, Louis, in her development, for Louis declares that "'We are going to open a school, and devote our lives to the upbuilding of the future race'" (73). Finally, Miriam's direct influence in Louis's life and her indirect influence in Minnie's life lead to Minnie's engagement in very specific service activities in the black community of newly freed slaves. Minnie's activities reflect her growth and development from the bowers of ease to the fields of labor, for "She did not content herself with teaching them mere knowledge of books. . . . It was her earnest desire to teach them how to make their homes bright and happy. She had found her work and they had found their friend" (74).

Another significant parallel can be drawn between the direct speech of the foremother, Mrs. Heston, and the mulatta heroine, Minnie. Both exhibit strength and determination through their use of the language. These qualities are evident in Mrs. Heston's response to her daughter's removal from school because of her color:

> "I made up my mind that I would leave the place. I said, 'Heston, let us leave this place; let us go farther west. I hear that we can have our child educated there, just the same as any other child.' At first my husband demurred, for we were doing a good business; but I said, 'let us go, if we have to live on potatoes and salt'" (47).

Mrs. Heston communicates clearly that justice is more important than economic gain and that access to education exceeds opportunity for income. The same moral fiber appears in Minnie's language when she talks to her husband about intemperance:

> "When I pass by the grog-shops that are constantly grinding out their fearful grist of poverty, ruin and death, I long for the hour when woman's vote will be leveled against these charnel houses; and have, I hope, the power to close them throughout the length and breadth of the land" (78-79).

Minnie's husband responds to her verbal expression of strength and determination, "'Why darling, I shall begin to believe that you are a strong-minded woman'" (79). Like Mrs. Heston, the foremother, Minnie, the mulatta heroine, communicates strength through direct discourse to bring about desired change.

It is interesting that Harper characterizes Minnie, the mulatta heroine, as one who is above the norm. Harper explains in the conclusion that she consciously draws the portrait of her mulatta protagonist to subvert the expected literary image of the mulatta character who chooses to pass and thus serves no useful purpose in the black community: "I conceived of one of that same class to whom I gave a higher, holier destiny; a life of lofty self-sacrifice and beautiful self-consecration" (91). Harper, however, does not identify a contributing source or a contributing influence which compelled Minnie to share her talents and skills with the masses. It is Mrs. Heston's authentic historical narrative that changes the course of Minnie's life and grandmother Miriam's voice of authority and counsel that directs Louis's course. As Louis and Minnie become one in marriage and one in their efforts to uplift the race, each has the benefit of the other's foremother.

MRS. HARCOURT'S TRIAL AND TRIUMPH

Mrs. Harcourt serves as Annette's foremother in Harper's *Trial and Triumph* (1888-89) even though her language is often harsh. Perhaps when the older black woman plays both the roles of grandmother and foremother, black women writers portray a seemingly harsh, older black woman whose language exposes her own flaws, while at the same time whose language influences her granddaughter and the mulatta heroine.

Although Annette's grandmother, Mrs. Harcourt, loves Annette, Annette is an unwelcome guest thrust upon Mrs. Harcourt—she is the product of the saddest experience of Mrs. Harcourt's life (191). A neighbor, Mrs. Lasette, seems to play a more significant role in Annette's life because she is a teacher of social graces, a listener, and an advisor. She is knowledgeable about Annette's past and is consistent in her support of Annette. She is a friend who understands Annette better than her grandmother does (185). The foremothering wisdom one might expect from the older woman thus seems on first reading to be displaced to a woman the age of Annette's deceased mother. Also having a daughter of her own, Mrs. Lasette seems better equipped to identify the heroine's needs and nurture her development.

Mrs. Harcourt provides Annette's basic needs but always voices harsh criticism:

> "I've scolded and scolded till my tongue is tired, whipping don't seem to do her a bit of good. . . . Sometimes when I get so angry with her that I feel as though I could almost shake the life out of her, the thought of her dying mother comes back to me. . . . I am afraid she is born for trouble. Nobody will ever put up with her as I do. She has such an unhappy disposition" (180).

Despite her previous experience in mothering, Mrs. Harcourt is not necessarily the wisest guide. She tells Annette directly: "'You do give me so much trouble. You give me more worry than all six children put together; but there is always one scabby sheep in the flock and you will be that one'" (184). Mrs. Harcourt's words cut deeply. The narrator says of Annette that "Her own grandmother had prophesied evil things of her. She was to be the scabby sheep of the flock. . . . Without intending it, Mrs. Harcourt had struck a blow at the child's self-respect" (184). Although Mrs. Harcourt somehow raised her own children to have confidence and pride (188), her harsh criticism of Annette seems counterproductive. Mrs. Harcourt confesses now that she is not capable of the wise guidance, the firm hand, and the loving heart that Mrs. Lasette assesses to be Annette's particular need. Mrs. Harcourt admits, "'I am afraid that I am not equal to the task'" (181).

Mrs. Harcourt's initial protests and limitations mask her foremotherly attributes, however. For example, Mr. Thomas, Annette's former teacher, states, "'I should, by all means, decide for the education of the race through its motherhood rather than through its teachers,'" yet Mrs. Harcourt responds, "'But we poor mothers had no chance. We could not teach our children'" (183). Like Mr. Thomas, Harper believes that the mother's role is more important than the church's or schoolteacher's role in the education of children (Foster 1990, 285). Mrs. Harcourt contends that poor mothers cannot teach their children. Yet being an uneducated, widowed mother of six, she "wanted each one to have some trade or calling" (189). Thus her desires and hopes, not textbooks, led her to nurture what she observed to be the "tastes and inclinations" of her children, who engaged in the skills and professions of farming, sewing, carpentry, medicine and teaching (190). Mrs. Harcourt, of course, teaches Annette and influences the positive development of Annette's life in important ways without knowing the significant role she is playing on a daily basis. For example, because Mrs. Harcourt must work to support herself and Annette, even her absence is a positive attribute. Annette is afforded the solitude to ponder life and race, and these reflections eventually lay the foundation of her passionate writing style.

More importantly, despite her negative criticism Mrs. Harcourt is the true foremother figure because her influence springs from the education of experience rather than the process of schooling. For example, when Annette speaks harshly about their neighbor, Mrs. Larkins, Mrs. Harcourt immediately admonishes her not to speak against an elder: "'Hush Annette, you must not talk that way of any one so much older than yourself. When I was a child I wouldn't have talked that way about any old person. Don't let me hear you talk that way again'" (184). She exhibits remnants of her traditional African roots, for to honor and show reference for elders is fundamental in traditional African culture. When Annette attempts to rationalize her own bad behavior, she recalls the words of the preacher, who taught about the wiles of the devil. Mrs. Harcourt counters by rendering an explication of the scripture without opening the bible when she explains to Annette that the devil only tempts human beings—he does not make them do bad things (183). Mrs. Harcourt is teaching unknowingly by virtue of the role she plays. Christian observes that in the past, the women of any group have represented the body of ideals by which that group measured itself; therefore, because the women bear and raise children, they have, for better or worse, embodied intangibles of a culture deemed worthy to be passed on more than any code of law or written philosophy (1985, 4).

Again, despite Mrs. Harcourt's harsh criticism of Annette, she responds angrily to a neighbor who has sent Annette to a saloon for beer (196). Her discourse reveals the protectiveness she feels for Annette and the desire to curb negative influences in her life. Although Mrs. Lasette teaches social graces, Mrs. Harcourt teaches resistance to social ills. Mrs. Lasette values the outer garment of social graces—the pragmatic facets of life that engage one on occasion, whereas Mrs. Harcourt cultivates the inner spirit that when exercised will be strong enough to resist the evils that bombard one day to day. To engage in social graces is desirable, but to be equipped to resist social ills is necessary for survival. Mrs. Harcourt's discourse not only affects the course of Annette's life but changes the life of the neighbor, who abandons intemperance after Mrs. Harcourt's reprimand:

> She told her in emphatic terms she must never do so again . . . that she ought to be ashamed of herself, not only to be guzzling beer like a toper, but to send anybody's child to a saloon. "I am poor, but I mean to keep my credit up and if you and I live in this neighborhood a hundred years you must never do that thing again" (196).

Yet another instance when Mrs. Harcourt defends Annette occurs when she confronts Mrs. Lasette: "'your Alice hardly ever comes to see Annette, and never asks her to go anywhere with her, but may be in the long run Annette will come out better than some who now look down upon her'" (231).

Just as Mrs. Harcourt defends Annette, the town of Tennis Court engages in a parallel activity. As is typical of most communities, the town of Tennis Court criticizes its residents, defines its heroes, heroines, and outcasts, and rallies behind its own. Although the community often whispers about Annette's appearance, forecasts a negative future for her, and feigns sympathy for her grandmother, Annette's graduation is symbolic of some level of success for every member of the community of Tennis Court. To have one of its own rising to the point of graduation makes a statement to those outside the community. In the context of other communities, Annette's graduation raises the community above its poor reputation, as well as above racial and class discrimination (239). Annette's individual achievement becomes a service to the community already, again connecting, as in works discussed earlier, the foremother's values to improvement of the race by the mulatta heroine. The community recognizes Annette's academic excellence and her spiritual growth, for the narrator indicates that Annette had entered the church, so her conduct toward others in the community had become friendlier (240). Maryemma Graham and Gina Rossetti claim that Harper creates this channel of righteous behavior and Christian values for her female characters so that they can resist inequitable treatment (1996, 303-304). It is the Christian values and discourse of the foremother, which, by example, resist social ills and exceed the roles of the church and school teacher when the language is permeated with foremotherly hope and desire.

Expressed and unexpressed desire, righteous behavior, Christian values, harsh criticism, community praise, and unavoidable solitude all contribute to the development of Annette's thoughtful and critical approach to life. This asset of critical thinking helps Annette to make the major decision to break her marital engagement with Clarence Luzerne because of his legal commitment to another. Annette's decision parallels the sacrificial action that Mrs. Harcourt took when she assumed the responsibility to raise Annette. It also parallels other facets of the foremother-heroine relationship that reveal the influence of the foremother in defining the heroine. Taking into consideration the community rather than her individual self, Annette does not permit Luzerne to divorce his long-lost ailing wife. She concludes that "'the great end to life is not the attainment of happiness but the performance of duty and the development of character. The great question is not what is pleasant but what is right'" (280). The voice of the foremother echoes in this conscientious sentiment; this summary statement of values of the heroine. As noted in the Conclusion of *Minnie's Sacrifice*, Harper consciously and purposefully constructs her characters in working explicitly against "the literature . . . from the hands of white men who would paint them in any colors which suited their prejudices or predilections" (239-240). Such a statement is textual evidence that Harper knowingly constructs her characters to refute stereotypical, clay-like figures, for her characters are inscribed with voice and values and consciousness and complexity. Mrs. Harcourt in *Trial and Triumph* is not a replica of Mrs. Heston in *Minnie's Sacrifice*, just as grandmother Miriam in *Minnie's Sacrifice* is not replicated by Aunt Linda in *Iola Leroy or Shadows Uplifted*. Each foremother is a distinct individual, sometimes flawed, who influences with varying levels of language whether it is direct or indirect in the context of the mulatta heroine.

AUNT LINDA IN *IOLA LEROY*

Aunt Linda, in Harper's last novel *Iola Leroy or Shadows Uplifted* (1892) shows the strength of the foremother in language use and deed, for she openly criticizes unscrupulous political and religious activities, maintains a discourse of uplift for the community of blacks, and articulates a vision for the future generation of blacks. Surprisingly, however, *Iola Leroy* appears to praise not the foremother figure of Aunt Linda but the stereotypical figure of Mammy Liza when she is credited for her faithfulness and careful attention to the Leroy children. Mammy Liza seems to be the muted foremother, more like the stereotypical mammy because of the slavery setting, while Aunt Linda emerges as the new full version of the foremother, subverting the stereotype, in the realm of the Civil War and freedom under Reconstruction.

Mammy Liza possesses the attributes of a typical mammy on a white plantation, for Iola (while she believes she is white) includes Mammy Liza in her discussion with classmates of the pros and cons of slavery: "'I love my mammy as much as I do my own mother, and I believe she loves us just as if we were her own children. When we were sick I am sure that she could not do anything more for us than she does'" (97). Mammy Liza serves as the typical mammy when she uses direct discourse to console Iola's mother, Marie Leroy, following the death of her husband: "'Oh honey, yer musn't gib up. Yer knows whar to put yer trus'.'" Mammy consoles and prays for Marie, as expected of a loyal servant: "kneeling by the side of her mistress she breathed out a prayer full of tenderness, hope and trust" (94). Finally, Mammy Liza holds faithful vigils at the death bed of Iola's younger sister, after the family has been remanded to slavery due to the revelation of Marie's mixed heritage: "The servants gathered around her with tearful eyes, as she bade them all good-bye. . . . Mammy had lowered the pillow" (108). Although Mammy Liza's voice is minimized in the text, as a typical mammy on a white plantation her presence is maximized. Iola's mother regrets that her children have interacted only with the slaves of the plantation, and she dreads the effect of such interaction upon their lives and character (82). Such an interaction, however, proves to have been a positive one, for it serves as a knowledge base—a foundation for the mental, emotional, and social transition Iola and her brother have to make when they learn of their mixed heritage. Viguerie observes that Mammy Liza virtually disappears from the text when the household changes from white to black (1993, 260). Her influence emerges minimally in the discourse through thought when Iola vividly reminisces about Mammy Liza when she is in the presence of the foremother, Aunt Linda. Mammy Liza, then, holds a residual influence in Iola's life because "There was something so motherly in Aunt Linda's manner that it seemed to recall the bright, sunshiny days when she used to nestle in Mam Liza's arms, in her own happy home" (169). Iola sees Aunt Linda, the foremother, and Mammy Liza, the stereotypical mammy, as one. This linkage of the mammy figure with the foremother is indicative of Iola's twoness, for the mammy figure of Mammy Liza triggers reminiscences of her white past, including a "white" girl's relationship to a black mammy, while the foremother figure of Aunt Linda evokes the mulatta heroine of the present. As stated previously in this study, the older black females characterized as foremothers in early black women's literature are often presumed to be the stereotypical mammy figure and therefore dismissed as such or accepted as a representative mainstay of the period. The fact that Aunt Linda is the true foremother is evident in her nature, language, and deeds, and is eventually reflected in the mulatta heroine's nature, language and deeds, despite Iola's initial failure to distinguish the two characters.

The foremother's cultural, familial, and maternal nature is meaningful. Elizabeth Young suggests that Harper feminizes the war narrative by using literary form to represent the importance of maternal and familial structures in the black community. In *Iola Leroy*, the Civil War, then, is filtered through a maternal lens (294). Young further points out that the black women play central roles in the Civil War, for Aunt Linda sells baked goods to soldiers, a black laundress serves as a spy, and Iola serves as a nurse (299). Aunt Linda plays yet other roles later as she filters the events of the Reconstruction period through a folk lens. In stark contrast to Mammy Liza, Aunt Linda is an activist who speaks against the whites who bring their liquor business to the black community (157). She knows the unfair practices that politicians use to gain the black vote (160), and she criticizes her own people for getting involved in the affairs of the dominant culture when they show interest only in the material and the political (162). In the many roles that Aunt Linda plays, her underlying concern is her vision for radical change for blacks occurring when young blacks take the helm. Iola hears Aunt Linda's words and later transforms vision and political desire into practical application.

Aunt Linda represents the articulation of a position through the channel of discourse—the filtering of experiences through the words of the figure who is now permitted voice and reflects the complexity of humanity. She reflects both negative and positive attributes that are confirming for the audience that shares the same cultural heritage. John Ernest comments on Harper's characterization by stating that one can hear the history best by listening to individual voices giving particular form to the complex cultural relations not only of the outside world but of that world which lies within (1995, 206). Aunt Linda's presence is meaningful, for she emerges at the beginning, in the middle, and at the end of the novel. Her voice articulates the wrongs of the past, the concerns of the present, and the visions for the future. Ernest comments further on the attributes of characterization: "Aunt Linda and Uncle Daniel, the two most prominent representatives of black 'folk' culture in the novel, completely uneducated by any dominant cultural standard of measurement, are capable of seeing 'visions' of events in both this world and beyond" (193). No one questions those who possess the spiritual gifts of vision and prophecy, for these gifts are expected to dwell in some human vessel within the community of black folks.

Iola's encounter with Aunt Linda is initially problemmatic, however, by differences of class and education. The foremother represents black folk culture, and the language reveals the dynamics of Aunt Linda's and Iola's somewhat hierarchical relationship. Unlike Iola's, Aunt Linda's voice dominates in a speech situation; she is the societal voice (157), the politically astute commentator (160), the harsh critic of religious leaders (161), and the savvy real estate business woman (173). Although Iola is educated by the standards of the dominant culture and is supposedly an ideal female to represent the black race in the uplift movement, this chapter later reveals how her voice is subordinate to Aunt Linda's voice in a speech situation within the community, with the result that her words seem inconsequential in this context, as opposed to their force in the conversations among the educated blacks. An example of the significance and influence of Aunt Linda's language occurs following her assessment of the destruction to human life during the period of Reconstruction. She professes, "'But I don't think dese young folks is goin' ter take things as we's allers done'" (171). Aunt Linda envisions that younger people will recognize the mechanisms of oppression and dismantle those mechanisms. Young people will participate in government, learn skills, buy their own businesses, buy their own land and homes, and meet discrimination with resistance, whether physical revolt or peaceful persistence, but cling to their cultural heritage and their familial roots. Iola's conversation with Aunt Linda becomes a learning experience that will have a tangible outcome in Iola's program of community action.

To maintain clarity in vision and purpose one must frequently return to one's roots. Rather than a return to her roots, Iola is faced with an introduction to and discovery of her roots when she journeys south. Carby observes that Harper uses the visit to the plantation to "acquaint" her heroine and her audience with the true nature of black folks as well as to define Iola's relation to the race (1987, 77). Clearly the foremother, Aunt Linda, is a representative of this black folk culture necessary to Iola's mature purpose in life. In the significant linkage between Aunt Linda and the mulatta heroine Carby points out Aunt Linda's strenuous argument, in support of the black community, that what is needed is leaders "'who'll larn dese people how to bring up dere chillen, to keep our gals straight, an' our boys from runnin' in de saloons an' gamblin dens'" (161). Although Carby claims that Harper creates Iola to play the role of intellectual leader (77), she later observes that the text inscribes Lucy Delaney and Reverend Carmicle with the attributes of intellectual leadership (91). It is within the context of the foremother, however, that discursive practices reveal more namely, that Iola's growth owes much to the foremother's influence as Iola clearly rises to the level of moral leader in the black community. Iola is explicit in her desire to work among her people. Elizabeth Young parallels Iola's refusal of Dr. Gresham's second proposal of marriage and her expressed wish to be among her people ("'I feel that our paths must diverge. . . . I intend spending my future among the colored people of the South'" [Harper 234]) with Aunt Linda's expressed desire to realize her freedom: "I wanted ter re'lize I war free an' I couldn't, tell I got out er de sight and soun' ob ole Miss'" (Harper 154) (Young 1995, 304). Young does not argue that Aunt Linda directly motivates Iola's refusal. Neither critic shows the older black woman as a direct source of motivation. Neither critic establishes that the older black woman is instrumental in defining the mulatta heroine so that she develops into some greater use for the community of black people. Both Carby and Young observe resistance to forms of white control in the language of Aunt Linda and Iola, but neither explores further correlations between the two figures that call for a closer look.

Regarding Iola's nature, discourse, and deeds, Christian views Iola as a cultural missionary and a source of light because Iola shares the knowledge that she acquires from the white race with the black race. Christian sees Iola's roles as informed by a commitment to the black race (1980, 29). Such an assessment is an adequate appraisal of one of the roles that Iola plays, yet it is debilitating for the black community if Iola is simply imposing the cultural aspects of education of one culture on that of another. It is only with a side-by-side presentation of both cultural traditions in education, that is, a plural presentation without the hierarchy of superior and inferior, that Iola's role as a cultural missionary can be deemed positive. Further, her portrayal as a source of light bears some semblance of Hentz's patriarchal white planter, Moreland, in *The Planter's Northern Bride*, who provides light for those in darkness, figuratively and literally. Nevertheless, if Iola is representative of a light among her people, then it is important to determine the cultural source of her light rather than to presume the source to be simply that she possesses an education that is representative of the dominant culture. Mammy Liza and Marie Leroy are familial and maternal respectively, yet neither can be recognized as a sustained source of influence in defining the character of the mulatta heroine, Iola Leroy.

Foster notes that few critics recognize that Iola is a revision of the tragic mulatta stereotype that her mother Marie represents. Marie is passive and accommodating and does not use her intuitive powers as a gauge to detect and steer herself out of the path of impending danger. Iola, in her construction as a revised model, possesses the insight to perceive impending danger and to steer away from that danger when she denies Dr. Gresham's proposals of marriage and a life of ease (1993, 184). Like Minnie, Iola speaks of thoughts and purposes that have come to her in the "shadow" that she would never have learned in the "sunshine" (114). John Ernest points out that the thoughts and purposes that come to one in the shadows are the products of experience, the benefits of the ministry of suffering facilitated by experience (1995, 193). Iola expresses indebtedness in serving the race (235) because the race has provided her with the economic means to an education as a white female; yet the realization of this indebtedness occurs only after her cognitive transformation to the status of a mulatta. As a white female, Iola was incapable of realizing this indebtedness. After having met the foremother, Aunt Linda, and the community of black folks in the South, and after having experienced discrimination in employment in the North, Iola resists Dr. Gresham's attempt to plant the seed of hierarchical class differences within the race when he tells her that her education makes her unfit to live among the folks in the black community (235). Because Iola has been "schooled" in the North and briefly "educated" among her people in the South, she sees her schooling not as a vehicle for individual upward mobility as Dr. Gresham does, but as a resource for group empowerment when she elects to serve the people whose free labor funded her schooling: "I am indebted to them for the power I have to serve them" (235).

Harper has created a socially acceptable image of a black woman in Iola—not just physical beauty, class, and education, but also a social conscience (Christian 1985, 73) that can be attributed to the foremother figure. The first three characteristics, on the other hand, are replicas of what the dominant society defines as socially acceptable. The issue of colorism thus arises. Harper certainly chooses to endow her heroine with features that reflect the dominant culture's definition of beauty, just as she chooses to inscribe black adoration for these features as it is conveyed in Tom Anderson's description of Iola: "Beautiful long hair comes way down her back; putty blue eyes, an' jis' ez white ez anybody's in dis place," (38). Are there motives for this portrayal other than Harper's own colorism or her conformity to white ideals? Christian concludes in her essay entitled, "The Uses of History: Frances Harper's *Iola Leroy, Shadows Uplifted* (1983), that Harper attempted to change her audience's view of the black woman, but in her attempt to do so she had to conform to the form of the romance novel and the view of womanhood during the time in which she wrote. She believes that such a conformity was not necessarily a reflection of the reality of black women's conditions (1985, 170). I would suggest that in presenting Iola as a model Harper does present reality in her use of the mulatta heroine as a compromise for romance novel expectations, but also in the realization of the link between an influence in the form of the foremother and the mulatta heroine. Whether intentional or not, Harper, like other early black women writers, inscribes these aspects in the narrative.

Hazel Carby reconsiders in an interesting way the significance of the mulatta represented in the narratives of the late nineteenth century. She argues against other critics of African American literature who dismiss the mulatta as a concession to a white audience (89). Carby suggests that the mulatta should be analyzed as a narrative device of mediation. She serves the functions of both a vehicle for an exploration of the relationship between the races and an expression of the relationship between the races (89). As a vehicle, the mulatta is the result of one race's total domination of another. The relationship that resulted in Iola's birth generally lies between the powerless black female and powerful white male (even if the image of rape is softened in this case by elevation of the black mother's status and by mutual respect and love). The mulatta is an expression of the relationship between the races because of her physical appearance. She can possess all the features of a white female in skin color, hair texture, eye color, and genteel manner, but if the records show or even if someone suspects a trace of her Negro heritage, she is deemed a Negro and treated accordingly. Extending Carby's narrative device of mediation, I suggest that the mulatta serves the function of a vehicle for an exploration of the relationship between the presumed stereotypical mammy (idealized by whites and despised by most blacks) and the developing and resulting mulatta heroine, who is no longer a replica of the dominant culture's definition of socially acceptable because of physical likeness, but a construction redefined according to black cultural influences because of her sustained relationship with the foremother and the black community.

Iola's journey south unites her with the black community but also reveals her separateness from the folk. She finds a resting place and internal calm in the presence of Aunt Linda, yet Harper carefully distinguishes Iola from Aunt Linda and the black folk of the community. Harper's discursive practices define the relationship not only between the foremother and the mulatta heroine, but between the heroine and other minor characters. The speech situation of particular interest occurs when Iola accompanies Robert to Aunt Linda's house for supper (164). It is her first encounter with Aunt Linda and this black community. During the initial conversation, none of the speech participants respond when Iola speaks. Iola's language is a soliloquy as she summarizes someone else's language into moral and anecdotal abstractions. In the speech situation where the participants are Aunt Linda or Uncle Daniel, neither responds to Iola's commentary, moral or anecdotal. For example, Uncle Daniel speaks to Robert about his former master's money that he vowed to protect during the War and comments, "'Yes, yer older, but I wouldn't put it pas' yer eben now, ef yer foun' out whar it war'" (166). Iola recites a moral by stating, "'Yes, they say "caution is the parent of safety."'" Uncle Daniel does not respond. A second example occurs when Uncle Daniel responds to

Robert's question about the study of theology. He says "'Look a yere, boy, I'se been a preachin' dese thirty years, an' you come yere a tellin' me 'bout studying yore ologies. I larn'd my 'ology at de foot ob de cross'" (168). Iola formulates yet another moral recitation for Uncle Daniel's statement when she says, "'the moral aspect of the nation would be changed if it would learn at the same cross to subordinate the spirit of caste to the spirit of Christ'" (168). Again, Uncle Daniel does not respond. In conclusion Iola's overall language style—not only her Standard English but her habit of turning these characters' concrete language of experience into moral and intellectual abstractions—does not lend itself to the black linguistic cultural harmony of call and response. Iola's language style is too formal; thus she is immediately set apart from members of the community, as one can audibly imagine the momentary silence following her moral soliloquy-like utterances. Although the dialogue meshes in the end, this initial conversation disjunct reveals Iola's outsider status.

Language style not only magnifies non-response from the members of the black community, but elicits response from Iola as a listener. Iola indeed sees the black folk of the community as different even though they share the same heritage. Her distance from the community shows in the narrative voice, which reveals that Iola is amused by Aunt Linda's speech: "Iola rode along, conversing with Aunt Linda, amused and interested at the quaintness of her speech and the shrewdness of her intellect" (175) (Carby 1987, 78). One who is a member of the community usually shares some features of the dialect and does not, then, view language variation so arresting that it is regarded as "quaint." Carby recognizes yet another expression of Iola's distance from the black folk: Iola's inability to share in the conversation about the experiences of slavery. Aunt Linda, Salters, and Uncle Daniel's experiences span decades, whereas Iola's is brief after growing up with white privileges. Iola can never fully share in their experiences because she did not live through those experiences; thus a gulf remains between them (78). Iola, then, is portrayed as a spectator—an anthropological investigator of black folk. At this point she is not yet fully receptive to the folk wisdom of the foremother.

As a black woman educated by experience and one who is culturally centered, the foremother knows what is best for black people in general, young black people in particular, and her grandson in particular. Aunt Linda is determined to "make a man" of her grandson, who lives in her and Salters's home. Great mothering is subsumed in

Aunt Linda's and Salters's making of a man, for Salters speaks of the steps his grandson must take outside the home when he explains that he must learn to work first and acquire education later if he is smart (172). Aunt Linda and Salters know what one must do in order to survive and thrive in their community, be it by physical or mental labor. Their concept of the making of a man incorporates the values and beliefs of the culture, for he is a man only if he reflects what they believe to be appropriate for their own community. Iola again renders a tentatively expressed soliloquy-like moral which only formalizes what Aunt Linda has already expressed: "'I hope he will turn out an excellent young man, for the greatest need of the race is noble, earnest men, and true women'" (172).

As noted above, Aunt Linda has already surveyed the needs of the community when she tells Robert, "'I wants some libe man to come down yere an' splain things ter dese people. I don't mean a politic man, but a man who'll larn dese people how to bring up dere chillen, to keep our gals straight, an' our boys from runnin' in de saloons an' gamblin' dens'" (160-61).

To serve the plot function of Iola's dramatic reversal upon revelation of her origin, Harper also needed to use a character who could pass for white, but she uses this passing motif in turn to make a political comment on the arbitrariness of racism.

As in Carby's earlier reference to Aunt Linda's articulation of the needs of the black community, and her suggestion that Harper created the character Iola to fill that need (77), the text reveals specific language that confirms my argument that the desires of the foremother are later definitively manifested in the language and deeds of the mulatta heroine. For example, following her marriage to Dr. Latimer, Iola responds to Aunt Linda's verbalization of the need for the community: "'Well, Aunt Linda, I am going to teach in the Sunday-school, help in the church, [and] hold mothers' meetings to help these boys and girls to grow up to be good men and women'" (276). Iola's discourse has now adopted Aunt Linda's concreteness and yielded her former tendency to abstract moral generalizations. Also, although Iola still speaks the standard variety of English, her status changes from visitor to member in the black community when she returns with her husband to work in the community. The discourse between Aunt Linda and Iola reflects this change because it flows naturally without soliloquy. The text reveals a noticeable change in action and speech.

Aunt Linda rushed up to Iola, folded her in her arms, and joyfully exclaimed: "I seed it in a vision dat somebody fair war comin' to help us."

"But, Aunt Linda, I am not very fair," replied Mrs. [Iola] Latimer.

"Well chile, you's fair to me" (275).

Another change is that Iola's previous attempts to manifest her longing to teach were thwarted twice; the first time negative detractors torched her school (147), and the second time poor health forced her to relinquish her teaching duties (200). Yet she tells Aunt Linda with confidence, "'I am going to teach.'" The reader later observes Iola resisting discrimination in her attempts to gain employment. Although Iola acquires and loses two positions of salesperson, she states, "'I am determined to win for myself a place in the fields of labor'" (208). It is through her resistance to discrimination that the white employer, Mr. Cloten, takes a stand and stifles any plans for racist action from his employees when he hires Iola, a black woman (211). Iola, as Aunt Linda predicts of the younger generation, does not accept discrimination but resists it through formal and informal education, and service.

Iola's language of service clearly integrates Aunt Linda's desire for true leadership in the black community. Aunt Linda criticizes the politician and the minister, whom the community sees as leaders; she calls for one who is a leader based not on title or formal education but on service, for she specifies the service that must be rendered: "'to learn dese people how to bring up dere chillen. . . '" (161). Iola's wish to serve her people emerges distinctly in her lengthy conversation with Dr. Gresham when she tells him why she cannot marry him: "'I must serve the race which needs me most'" (235); I must "'do all in my power to help them'" (234); and "'I am indebted to them'" (235). It is this commitment to service, formal and informal education within the home and community, that links Harper's works with those of minor nineteenth-century black women writers Johnson, Kelley, and Tillman. Harper shares with Jacobs the conviction that along with education, the struggle for freedom and justice are ongoing, and that uplifting the race is not the work of the mulatta heroine alone, but also the constant workings of the ever-present foremother, who emerges in early black female works as the impetus of the heroine's values.

The early black female works studied thus far communicate serious messages that instill and strengthen the values and beliefs that inspire and uplift the family, community, and society of black people as a whole. Moving toward the early twentieth century and away from slavery and Reconstruction, one expects the literature to reflect more economic opportunity, equitable treatment, greater access to education, and less focus on the culturally-wise foremother and socially-conscious mulatta heroine. Surprisingly, however, at the turn of the century, Pauline Hopkins inscribes in her texts every black female stereotypical figure ranging from mammy and sapphire to wench and tragic mulatta. In her presentation of these stereotypical female figures, the values of the dominant culture become central and detailed in character while the values of the black culture become peripheral and blurred in comedy.

CHAPTER 5

Aunt Henny and Aunt Hannah in the Novels of Pauline Hopkins

It is interesting to see how the older black woman forges through physical and behavioral stereotypical features to emerge as foremother in the slave narrative and early black female fiction. It is also interesting to observe under what constraints she operates to continue her role as counselor, healer, and keeper of the traditions of the culture. Of Pauline Hopkins's four novels *Contending Forces* (1900), *Hagar's Daughter* (1901-02), *Winona* (1902) and *Of One Blood* (1902-03), I will study the serialized novels of *Hagar's Daughter* and *Of One Blood* primarily because both contain interesting variations of the foremother figure and secondarily because both works contain elements of the mystery novel and thus differ from the domestic novels and slave narrative selected for this study. I choose not to include Hopkins's extensive work *Contending Forces* because the older black woman figure which is most closely portrayed as a foremother figure (Mrs. Willis) actually emerges as a race woman. Her prominence as a race women, and an advocate and spokesperson for the black race places her in the foreground and thus in a different function than the foremother. Regardless of the narrative structuring principles of slave narrative, domestic fiction or serialized mystery, the foremother figure resides in most works of early black women writers. She subverts the stereotypical mammy found in early white female works even though she is often draped with the embellished, superficial features of the stereotype. Because she is complex, however, the foremother figure transcends the superficial. For example, in Pauline Hopkins's *Hagar's Daughter: A Story of Southern Caste* the foremother, Aunt Henny, possesses a humorous yet serious nature, adheres to yet deviates from standards, teaches yet remains uneducated, expresses ignorance yet possesses knowledge. She deserves public praise yet receives public blame. She is constrained by stereotypical features, yet she is clothed in her right mind.

AUNT HENNY AND HAGAR

Pauline Hopkins's novel *Hagar's Daughter: A Story of Southern Caste* (1901-02) provides examples of the stereotypical images that emerge in the works of early black women writers and co-exist with discourses of liberation. This co-existence appears contradictory, given that stereotypical constructs are created by members of the dominant culture and used for the purposes of maintaining the hierarchy of superior and inferior while creating economic profit to benefit themselves. Hopkins has benefitted little, but has elicited much criticism from this seeming contradiction between the use of stereotypical images and discourses of liberation.

While the main events of *Hagar's Daughter* revolve around the central character's (Hagar's) life—a life of outward disguise, intrigue, class consciousness, and materialism, the life of the black folks is also rich, but that richness is subdued by stereotypical characterization. Kristina Brooks says that "in objectifying some of her African American characters, Hopkins presents a sideshow—a minstrel show—to the main act" (134). I disagree in part with Brooks's assessment because underlying it is the implication that the real or serious action of the novel is that which models the dominant culture. Variations in behavior and language are easily defined as something outside the norm; therefore, these characterizations become subordinate to something or someone of greater importance. Difference is thus deemed deficient and relegated to the periphery by the one who holds the power to define. Arguably, aspects of Hopkins's black characterization, such as specific features of the language variation, are realistic. The problem is that specific features of language variation are stigmatized by members of the dominant culture. When these variations emerge, then the language, the character, and the culture are swept to the periphery and defined as a "side show to the main act." For example, Isaac's variety of language is fitting for Brooks's definition of a side show when he sincerely attempts to convince his wife, Marthy, "'Wha' you tink I'se turned over a new leaf fo' ef it warn't to see them chilluns holdin' up dar heads 'long wif de bes' ob de high-biggotty Wash'nt'n 'stockracy?'" (177). The reading audience might assume that Hopkins's attempt to write oral variations of the English language is to elicit the humor expected to be associated with such a character. It is not, however, the varied lexical forms which are problematic but the underlying meaning. Isaac communicates the impression that all blacks are class conscious and aspire to the materialistic values of the dominant culture. Hopkins's message, then, is consistent in that both those who can move in and out of the white society at will because of the disguise of passing, and those who cannot do so because of obvious color, still possess similar desires of success and assimilation.

Another example of variation in behavior and language occurs in the character of Isaac's daughter, Venus. Her behavior would likely warrant humor during her meeting with Detective Henson when "Venus showed her dazzling teeth in a giggle. She ducked her head and writhed her shoulders in suppressed merriment" (227). Venus is, in fact, educated by the dominant society's standards and even Detective Henson notes her "extremely intelligent, wide-awake expression" (223). Venus, however, represents the mental twoness of the oppressed when she reveals her knowledge of the pragmatic aspects of language use upon meeting Detective Henson, but reverts to the norm of the dialect of her community when she becomes emotionally distraught and "forgot her education in her earnestness, and fell into the negro vernacular, talking and crying at the same time" (224).

Isaac and Venus are clearly the stereotypical buck and simpleton, respectively, yet the harshest criticism of Hopkins's use of stereotypes has not, however, been leveled at the wench in the form of young Marthy, who readily accepts Isaac's sexual advances, when "Isaac improved the time between the going and coming of Aunt Henny by making fierce love to Marthy, who was willing to meet him more than half way" (44); or the Buck in the form of Isaac, who is the loyal comic: "'Dar neber was a better man den ol' massa an' I orter know. Lawse, de times me an' young massa had t'gedder bar hunts, gamblin' 'bouts. We bin like brudders'" (177). It is the mulatta heroine in the form of Hagar, who embraces the values and possesses the physical characteristics of the dominant culture, that results in the harshest criticism of Hopkins's work. Critic Jane Campbell refers to Hopkins's description of whites as "the higher race" (*Contending Forces* 23) when she argues that "blatant endorsement of racial supremacy has been responsible, in part, for the critical neglect of Hopkins's fiction."

Specifically, Campbell notes, "Hopkins hazards the idea that racial intermixture with Anglo-Saxons, however much it exploits women, has improved Afro-Americans, infusing blacks with characteristics of 'the higher race'" (1986, 40). I would speculate that the ease with which Hopkins uses the phrase "higher race" is similar to the contemporary use of the lexical forms "majority" and "minority," that is , "majority" is synonymous with the concept of the dominant race—the race that maintains positions of power. "Higher race" does not assume Hopkins's endorsement of white supremacy, nor does her use of the phrase confirm notions of colorism. Hopkins's *Hagar's Daughter* provides numerous examples that allude to improvement due to race mixing and that reflect the materialistic values and physical characteristics of the dominant culture. Senator Bowen's conversation with his wife Estelle (Hagar) reflects the materialistic values: "'There, Mrs. Senator, there's your diamond star you've been pining after for a month'" (88); and later at the ball in the Bowen mansion she appears "in white velvet, old lace, and diamonds" (111). The narrator describes Hagar's physical characteristics in her younger years: "pure creamy skin" (35) and "a fair vision in purest white" (53). Despite these explicit examples, however, Campbell observes that Hopkins still insists that people of African descent identify with their culture (40). Such contradictions cause tension in Hopkins's works. The author establishes clearly that a temporary means of social and economic attainment in white society is possible through conscious or unconscious disguise, where physical features and behavioral traits are identical to those of the dominant culture. Hopkins's work also reveals that to identify with African origins is to forego the benefits of white society by removing oneself outside the boundaries of a nation that still harbors the legacy of slavery.

Both Trudier Harris and Molefi Asante agree that character portrayal and discursive practices associated with portrayal are indicative of a writer's commitment. With the integration of stereotypical characterization and the advocacy of cultural pride in her texts, Hopkins promotes the seemingly conflicting patterns of perpetuating stereotypes, embracing white values, and promoting traditional cultural pride. After multiple close readings and numerous discussions, I am compelled to conclude that Hopkins uses black folk and their lives not to perpetuate stereotypes but to construct contrasts in order to depict obvious differences. Hopkins exaggerates dialect and behavior to illuminate the impossibility of disguise for her darker characters. At the same time Hopkins emphasizes language and behavior to magnify the possibility of disguise, and the ease with which near white characters can navigate the color line undetected. Hopkins does not create difference to perpetuate deficiency even though she drapes her darker characters in the familiar garments of stereotype. Hopkins's choices are indicative of her commitment, for example, when she places Aunt Henny in the Treasury Department of the United States.

Claire Pamplin explains that Hopkins wished for full opportunities for African Americans. She believed that those who demonstrate intelligence should be permitted to hold their rightful places in middle-class American life (1995, 170). Pamplin's argument is compelling, yet Hopkins's notions of "opportunities" still seemingly endorse the standards of the dominant culture. For example, Hopkins can be criticized for her portrayals of class consciousness in her heroines, Hagar, and her daughter, Jewell, in *Hagar's Daughter*, and both heroine and hero, Dianthe and Reuel in *Of One Blood*. She also seems to criticize Hagar's drive for "white" status at the expense of connection to her roots, and Hagar herself feels emotionally bereft amid her finery. On the other hand, although Hopkins drapes the mantle of class consciousness, cultural values, and physical features of the dominant culture on her mixed-race characters, she does not do so for the figure of the foremother.

Hopkins's *Hagar's Daughter* inscribes the unassuming foremother figure, Aunt Henny, with intelligence but without formal schooling. Aunt Henny, using her eloquent variety of the language, explains in a Court of Law: "'I seed dat villyun drap somethin' white inter de glass an' then turn 'roun' an' han' it to Miss Bradford'" (255). If intelligence is the act of understanding and the effective application of knowledge, then Aunt Henny's knowledge exceeds the knowledge of all those who were schooled according to the standards of the dominant culture—the lawyer, the Judge, the jury—when she effectively applies knowledge to expose misdeeds and unveil disguise. Aunt Henny successfully captures the attention of the Court when she unravels the mystery surrounding the Treasury Building murder. Yet, since those in the position of power can control images at will, the Attorney-General publicly distorts Aunt Henny's image of integrity and thereby her message of truth when he defines her words as "idiotic ramblings" and her very being as "an ignorant nigger." The Attorney-General chooses, on the other hand, to select patriotic lexical items such as "brilliant soldier" and "brave gentleman," indicative of white males, for the guilty General Benson (257). This scene certainly refutes the notion that the mammy receives patriarchal protection. Viguerie believes that black authors intentionally manipulate the mammy image to refute such notions as protection (231). Because of her assertiveness, decisiveness, and independence the older black woman is really perceived as a challenge to those in power (Jewell 1993, 7). It is those in power who define and influence the masses; therefore, the Attorney-General has determined that Aunt Henny is no longer to be regarded as a credible witness in a Court of Law. That role of credible witness is assumed by the white male hero, Detective Henson, who repeats Aunt Henny's message using a standard variety of her language and confirms that "'what she had said concerning General Benson is absolutely true'" (260). Hopkins challenges racist ideology and thereby supports Tate's belief that nineteenth-century sentimental narratives are discourses of liberation, but she maintains racial hierarchy in the courtroom scene in *Hagar's Daughter*. A similar paradox occurs in the use of white "authenticating" narratives to frame slave narratives such as Harriet Jacobs's or Mary Prince's. The courtroom scene could very well be Hopkins's depiction of the irony in a speech situation that compels whites to "authenticate" any truth spoken by blacks. Yet, the seeming contradiction to which Tate, Campbell, and others allude remains.

Although surrounded by recurring contradiction, racial tension, and character disguise, Aunt Henny possesses a stable identity, consistent language style, and, most importantly, a view of the world that confirms the character of the foremother. Even situated at the seat of government, surrounded by unscrupulous affairs, and in a world of status-seeking upper-class blacks who are passing, Aunt Henny remains unchanged. She is unchanged because she remains connected to her community and family. She labors endlessly to meet needs (Marthy's owning her own home) and to support aspirations (Oliver's attending college) so that the family and the community will thrive. Kristina Brooks argues in support of Hopkins's use of the mammy figure in that she perceives that the novel's white and mixed-race characters appear to need some such reality against which to stake their shifting identities and roles (1996, 144-45). Brooks, like other critics and readers, readily views Aunt Henny as the stereotypical mammy. Such an assumption confirms that my process of re-vision is necessary in order to distinguish the older black woman figure which perpetuates the stereotypical mammy in early black female fiction from the older black woman figure which subverts it.

In her earlier role of servant for the Sargeant family, Aunt Henny seems more like the stereotypical mammy. She develops a close working relationship with Hagar when Hagar performs specific household duties:

> Aunt Henny, a coal-black Negress of kindly face, brought in the little brass-bound oaken tub filled with hot water and soap, and linen towels. . . . It was [Hagar's] duty to wash the heirlooms of colonial china and silver. . . . they were dried only by her dainty fingers, and carefully replaced in the cupboard (33).

Aunt Henny's close association and long history with both the Sargeant and Enson families are reflected in her knowledge of the details of the mysterious circumstances surrounding the birth of St. Clair Ellis (63), who is approximately seven years Hagar's senior. When Hagar's adoptive mother dies, Hagar is left in her home with her servants—of whom only Aunt Henny is identified (39). Brooks sees Aunt Henny as an important substitute mother to Hagar (146), because she was a long-time servant in the Sargeant household from Hagar's childhood to young adulthood, and follows Hagar to the neighboring Enson Hall after her marriage to Ellis Enson. Mothering, however, is simply one of the many roles of the foremother. In her role as cook, "Aunt Henny now reigned supreme in the culinary department of the Hall. Her head was held a little higher, if possible, in honor of the new dignity that had come to the family from the union of the houses of Enson and Sargeant" (40). In this role, Aunt Henny, like the mammy figures examined previously in early white women's works, uses her work as an instrument by which to measure her authority and worth. In her role as protector, Aunt Henny shows concern about the ritual of ceremony. She is concerned that Mrs. Sargeant's funeral and Hagar Sargeant and Ellis Enson's wedding occur too closely together. Furthermore, Aunt Henny's role of protective mammy is particularly strong when she is more protective of Hagar (her once young white charge turned mistress) than her own daughter when she admonishes Marthy not to spread Enson family secrets. Aunt Henny is first slave—slave in the sense of loyal caregiver to Hagar—then mother to Marthy (Brooks 1996, 141). Kimberly Wallace-Sanders's conclusion is similar in her examination of the literary depiction of the relationship between the black female slave/servant and white children, in comparison with the slave's and servant's regard for their own children. Wallace-Sanders holds that whether the older black woman is portrayed as slave, mammy, or servant, her mothering role is superseded by the role of family member within the white household (4). Whether by force of circumstance or by choice, Aunt Henny fulfills the expected behavioral characteristics of the mammy.

In her initial portrait as slave in the Sargeant and Enson households, on the other hand, Aunt Henny possesses the attribute of knowing from a historical perspective, a cultural perspective, and a spiritual perspective. Even in her protective role, Aunt Henny shows her reliance on traditional African cultural practices when she seeks the skills of Uncle Demus to obtain the charm that would steer evil away from Hagar. Uncle Demus pronounces that, "'Long as yer mistis keep dis 'bout her trouble'll neber stay so long dat joy won't conquer him in de end'" (41). When Marthy hears Aunt Henny repeat these words, she is impressed and looks at her mother in awe. Aunt Henny's own daughter exhibits high regard for the knowing nature of the foremother. Aunt Henny knows what Hagar's major problems will be when she utters, "'My young Miss will be all right ef dat St. Clair Enson keeps 'way from hyar,'" (41). Revealing her historical perspective, she utters upon Isaac's arrival, "'I ain't fergit nuffin'"(42); also "nobody knows dat Marse St. Clar an' Isaac better'n I does. I done part raise 'em bof'" (47). Her intuitive nature emerges when she says to Isaac, "'No use yer lyin' ter me, Isaac, yer Aunt Henny was born wif a veil. I knows a heap o' things by seein' 'em fo' dey happens. I don't tell all I sees, but I keeps up a steddyin' 'bout it'" (43). The foremother, Aunt Henny, was born with a caul and hence the gift of second-sight; therefore she sees and thus knows. She sees with full understanding, as Jacobs's Aunt Nancy in *Incidents* could see that nothing was more relevant to the enslaved than freedom, and Harper's Aunt Linda in *Iola Leroy* could see that politicians and religious leaders were not the true leaders for black people. It is with this gift of full understanding that Aunt Henny plays the role of messenger in the Enson household during the critical period when Hagar's mixed heritage is revealed to her husband. Aunt Henny is fully aware of the threat and coercion that had invaded the Enson household through familial ties (55), yet she chooses knowingly to say nothing when Marthy tells her that Hagar "done gone clean destructed" after hearing of her mixed heritage (57).

Hagar, the mulatta heroine, does not respond to the knowledge of her mixed heritage as past heroines, such as Minnie in Harper's *Minnie's Sacrifice* and Iola in *Iola Leroy*, who experience emotional and physical shock, but move beyond the shock to acceptance over time. Hagar engages in the discourse of stereotypical interior monologue when she is confronted with the discovery of her mixed heritage: "Was she, indeed, a descendant of *naked black savages* of the *horrible African jungles*? She examined her features in the mirror, but even to her prejudiced eyes there was not a trace of the *despised chattel*" (57 emphasis added). Hagar's language reflects that of the dominant culture as she is fitted with the uncomfortable lens of double consciousness and sees her blackness as it is perceived through the eyes of whites. She knows and therefore uses only the language of her oppressor. Claire Pamplin observes that Hagar, like Hopkins's subjects in general, reclaims her blackness in her "acknowledgement" of its existence, but she soon eagerly re-embraces her whiteness and the social, economic, and political advantages that it yields. Such actions result in narrative strategies which contribute to the complex and contradictory nature of Hopkins's works (176). Following Hagar's verbal and emotional reaction to her mixed heritage, she engages in physical pro-action and escapes enslavement by jumping over a bridge with her baby, readily accepting the belief that her baby dies as a result. Hagar survives and deliberately passes for white when she begins a new life in California as Hagar Marks (81). It is reasonable to assume that after the Civil War, Hagar could elect to work for the uplifting of her race, as Harper's Minnie Le Croix and Iola Leroy choose to do. Hagar does not. Major contributing factors are the temporary absence of the foremother figure, Aunt Henny, and the permanent absence of Hagar's biological mother, about whom the reader knows nothing other than that she was enslaved. The maternal ties that bind are slack, so Hagar experiences no yearning for pleasant, nurturing childhood experiences, as Iola did. Rose Valley holds only vague unpleasant memories for Hagar (57); her memories of Aunt Henny apparently unable to compete with her shocking discovery, the assumed death of her child, and her desire to be assimilated into wealth and status. The measurable influence of the biological mother and the overwhelming influence of the foremother were major factors which contributed to defining the part that Minnie and Iola would play in uplift of the race. These necessary proddings are weak in Hagar's life. On the other hand, although Hagar embraces the values of the dominant culture after acknowledging her mixed heritage, the text reveals how the threads of influence of the foremother figure are nevertheless interwoven into her life.

Aunt Henny, the foremother and representative of the black race, has had a measurable influence on Hagar's life. For example, during Hagar's prolonged wait for her husband's return to their Enson home, it is Aunt Henny who spends most of her spare time praying and coaxing Hagar out of the apathy into which she has fallen (63). Again Aunt Henny is in close proximity to Hagar during critically emotional periods of her life; the first is the death of her mother and the second is the threat of losing her husband, which would result in her and her child's being remanded to slavery after the revelation of her mixed heritage. It is in the midst of the latter critically emotional period that Hagar's voice parallels Aunt Henny's in character assessment and tone when she makes the accusation: "'You [St. Clair] are his murderer! You are his slayer'" (70-71). Aunt Henny's discourse had previously revealed the demonic nature of St. Clair when she told her daughter, Marthy, "'ef de debbil ain't de daddy den dat ol' rapscalion neber had a borned servant in dis sinful wurl'" (64). Aunt Henny remains steadfast in her opinion of St. Clair.

Aunt Henny's character as a whole remains unchanged even though Hagar's outward identity shifts. Twenty years after Hagar escapes from slavery and assumes another identity in California, her innocent, youthful longings come to fruition: "She longed to mix and mingle with the gay world; She [Hagar] had a feeling that her own talents, if developed, would end in something far different from the calm routine of housekeeping and church which stretched before her" (33). Hagar is no longer the country maiden turned tragic mulatta, but is disguised as the very white Estelle Bowen, who now resides in the midst of the gay world of Washington, D. C. Hopkins selects the effective motif of passing not only as a disguise for intrigue, but as a mechanism to blur the division between the black and white races. Hopkins uses disguise to show that it works on the level of appearance, but that the inner nature of the character does not change (Carby 1987, 146-47).

Aunt Henny upon first reading seems to be the stereotypical mammy. My earlier close reading, however, brings out Aunt Henny's gift of insight about human character, thus adding to the credibility of her stature as foremother. Her insight, like the word, possesses a generative power because both Marthy and Estelle Bowen (Hagar) exhibit some form of this power. For example, Marthy exhibits this intuitive gift when she links Aunt Henny's disappearance with her dream. She admits, "'It's borne in on me that sumthin' is wrong'" (172). Even Detective Henson comments on the significance of insight when he says to Jewel, "'I have confidence in intuitive deductions'" (190). Most important is the evidence of Estelle Bowen's (Hagar's) intuitive awareness when she immediately senses danger upon meeting Major Madison's daughter, Aurelia Madison (107). The rich and beautiful Aurelia Madison is also of mixed black and white heritage and is passing as white. Like Hagar, Aurelia was separated from her biological slave mother; however, Aurelia lies in stark contrast to Hagar because she was raised by her mother's former slave master (158-59) without the benefit of the foremother presence Hagar had. Thus, Hagar experiences doubt deep in her heart when she hears Aurelia's story about her past acquaintance with Jewel Bowen's fiance, Cuthbert Sumner (136). Estelle verbalizes her feelings to her daughter Jewell when she explains, "'but I believe her false. I have a presentiment that there is something wrong'" (137). Knowing, intuitive awareness, and spiritual insight are significant motifs in *Hagar's Daughter*, for even the villain, General Benson, "felt uneasy in her [Hagar's] presence, that under her haughty manner a keen insight was hidden that read his motives" (139).

Yet despite Hagar's intuitive strength, she follows the values of the white world as Estelle Bowen. Estelle (Hagar) reveals an aspect of her own character after Jewell defends her action to marry the accused murderer, Sumner. Estelle says to her daughter, "'What a champion you are, Jewell; once, perhaps, I should have acted and felt as you do. Now, my child, I am of the world'" (193). One can deduce from Estelle's words that her own selection of mate is based upon the expected social and economic outcome for herself, not emotion:

> The Senator fell in love with her immediately and at the end of a week proposed marriage.... She accepted his offer, vowing he should never have cause to regret his act. One might have thought from her eager acceptance that in it she found escape, liberty, hope (81).

How others respond to Estelle Bowen (Hagar) confirms her repression of feeling. Estelle's party guests see her as beautiful, yet their descriptions are consistently followed by the adversative conjunction, *but*: "'She is really a beautiful woman, *but* too cold to please me" (113); "Granted she is beautiful *but* she looks a creature of snow and ice'" (114).

Such discourse of adversatives assists in defining the mulatta heroine, where the language of the foremother is lacking in such definition. It is again Aunt Henny's overall long-term presence and her role, more than words, that are instrumental in defining the tenuous foremother-mulatta relationship in *Hagar's Daughter*. After Aunt Henny's and Jewell's release from captivity, they gather in Estelle Bowen's private parlor with no respect of class or race: "Anyone who had entered the room would have been surprised at the kind solicitude and graciousness shown old Aunt Henny who was an honored guest" (240). This reunion of Aunt Henny and Estelle Bowen (Hagar) is evidence of the influence of the foremother figure, for although the two were separated temporally and spatially, Aunt Henny's aura of significance exists even if unspoken during this period of reunion. Aunt Henny's influence is more evident when Estelle and Jewell Bowen decide not to enter the courtroom again until Aunt Henny testifies (243). Aunt Henny is the key to exposing false identities when she plays the role of trustworthy historian. Yet, as the above courtroom scene reflects, truth is subordinate to social opinion when the message and the messenger are pushed to the brink of peripheral silence.

Whether a figure of silence or one of minimal voice, the foremother figure remains through the tension between stereotypical images and discourses of liberation. Not only her presence but her role during critically emotional periods in the mulatta heroine's life are over-arching. Aunt Henny's roles as protector, counselor, seer, judge of character, and witness to character reveal many of her foremotherly attributes. The foremother's commitment to family and community is readily apparent; thus in Hopkins's creation of Aunt Henny, she shows commitment to social advancement because among other things Aunt Henny's action and location consistently shatter the general stereotypical myths that blacks are untrustworthy and lazy. Trudier Harris says that most black writers who create maids in their fiction do so with some goal in mind such as the social advancement of blacks in general (1982, xiv). Hopkins's placing Aunt Henny, then, in the Treasury Department of the United States is socially significant. Aunt Henny holds the life-long position of a maid because of her proven honesty regarding the handling of a large sum of money; however, not only her extraordinary act of honesty but the place itself, as a symbol of available money and national importance, contradict the pervasive myth of theft. The portrait of Aunt Henny is also socially significant because it reveals commitment to social advancement when she promotes economic development and educational attainment within her own community.

AUNT HANNAH AND DIANTHE

Like many contemporary black women writers (e.g., Toni Cade Bambara and Gloria Naylor), Pauline Hopkins incorporates in her works avenues of knowing and being that contradict the rational, the western, and the scientific. She incorporates the psychic phenomena, dream analyses, past life glances, visions, signs, ancient wisdoms, and root men (Hull 220). Along with *Hagar's Daughter* Hopkins's novel *Of One Blood or the Hidden Self* (1902-03) represents one of these avenues of being and knowing. It is not until the end of the novel that Dianthe, the mulatta heroine, meets Aunt Hannah, the foremother, who appears to be expecting her: "An opening in the trees gave a glimpse of cultivated ground in a small clearing, and a few steps further revealed a typical Southern Negro cabin, from which a woman stepped out and faced her as if expecting her coming" (603). Aunt Hannah possesses intuitive knowledge and actual historical knowledge, for "she was very aged, but still erect and noble in form. The patched figure was neat to scrupulousness, the eye still keen and searching" (603). Although the narrator shares the foremother's name during what appears to be the introduction of Aunt Hannah and Dianthe, the text alludes to a previous meeting where the name is suppressed. For it was with a woman in a small cottage that Dianthe spent many weeks following the canoe accident that resulted in the death of Aubrey Livingston's fiancee and Dianthe's friend, Molly Vance. The narrator says that "staggering like a drunken man, [Aubrey] made his way to a small cottage up the bank, where a woman, *evidently expecting him*, opened the door without waiting for his knock. For weeks after these happenings Dianthe lived in another world, unconscious of her own identity" (596-97 emphasis added).

The narrator explains that Dianthe "seemed again to have lost her own will in another's" (603) when Aunt Hannah invites her into her southern cabin. Brooks calls this state "objectivity" because it consists of being acted upon, as an object. Dianthe is shrouded in objectivity because she appears to have no will of her own. Brooks defines "subjectivity" first as the literary critical notion of the well-rounded character who conveys individuality and personhood. She defines it secondly as the feminist theoretical perspective of a classically male position of having a point of view, acting upon the world, while the classically female position of being objectified entails being acted upon and rendered a nonsubject (1996, 150 n. 6). Thus, Dianthe is an example of objectivity because she has held no point of view due to her mental disorientation. She is prone to lapse into trances and cannot recall her past. Dianthe lacks individuality because she is dependent on the friendship of Molly Vance for her well-being, and because she is repeatedly acted upon by others. Reuel Briggs subjects her to hypnosis, and Aubrey Livingston pursues and ultimately possesses her. It is only after she visits Aunt Hannah and hears the story of her heritage that Dianthe makes decisions on her own and acts upon the world around her. I propose that Aunt Hannah is the agent in this rescue: "An old black woman rescues Dianthe and immediately recognizes that she is her daughter Mira's child."[1] "'Gawd-a-mercy! My Mira's gal! My Mira's gal!'" (604). During this significant rescue mission and meeting, Dianthe accepts Aunt Hannah's declaration that she is of mixed heritage. She learns that both her grandmother Hannah and her mother Mira were "raped black mothers."[2] Dianthe learns further that she is the product of a triangular incestuous relationship, since she is married to both of her brothers, Reuel Briggs, who was thought to have died in Africa, and Aubrey Livingston. As the foremother, Aunt Hannah knows and shares the family history. Dianthe suffers emotionally from the revelation of the truth and literally chooses death when her brother and husband, Aubrey Livingston, forces her to drink the poisoned liquid she has prepared for him.

Hopkins chooses black folks to communicate the truth to both the mulatta heroine, Dianthe, and the mulatto hero, Reuel. Dianthe learns the truth from her foremother and grandmother, Aunt Hannah, and Reuel from Jim Titus, a traveling companion. Now that Aunt Hannah has provided the link to Dianthe's past, the dying mulatta heroine and tragic mulatta longs for Aunt Hannah's presence: "She would call her maid; but, no, her cold, unimpassioned face would bring no comfort to her aching heart, aching for pity, for some cheering bosom, where she might sob her ebbing life away" (613). Dianthe's longing prompts Aunt Hannah's immediate appearance. It is as though there were life-affirming contacts between the two people—like physical strands connecting them (Brooks 1996, 133). Dianthe responds intensely to

Aunt Hannah's entrance: "'O joy!' old Aunt Hannah's arms enfold her. For hours the two sat in solemn conference, while the servants wondered and speculated over the presence of the old witch" (613). "Old Aunt Hannah, with a fortitude born of despair, ministered in every possible way to the dying girl" (616). Unlike Harper's Iola Leroy, who talks about her plans to search for her mother and embarks upon a mission to do so, Dianthe verbalizes no such plans. Dianthe's mother, Mira, visits her in spirit. Reuel, who embarks upon an expedition for financial gain, literally falls into the bosom of their ancestral lineage, reflecting Hopkins's unique variation on the search for and discovery of family (Carby 1987, 157).

Dianthe, like the foremother, Aunt Hannah, possesses the ability to experience visually and aurally what others do not, for she hears the arrival of Reuel's entourage before anyone else. Like Aunt Hannah, Dianthe is expecting him: "'Still they have a long mile to traverse. O, Hasten! They call me home.'. . . Then winding her cold arms around his neck, she laid her weary head upon his shoulder and silently as the night passed through the portals of the land of souls" (616). Dianthe takes complete control of the world around her by delaying her death until Reuel's arrival. She becomes a subject instead of an object even if her agency is expressed not in life but in death.

Aunt Hannah's significance is clinched when Reuel returns with her to the ancient Hidden City on the continent of Africa. Aunt Hannah is willing to accompany him, for she has always maintained her spiritual connectedness to her African origins. She has served her purpose in the foreign land of America, for through her spirituality and meaningful language Dianthe has found freedom in the knowledge of her mixed heritage. Reuel has fought to conceal his mixed heritage, but eventually both Reuel and Dianthe find freedom through knowledge. Both are free of imposed and contrived constraints of the white world because Dianthe finds freedom through the foremother and then death, and Reuel finds freedom not only in accepting the knowledge of his black heritage, but in cherishing it. Reuel spends the remainder of his life as African royalty with Queen Candace, who has jet black hair and a warm bronze complexion, and his grandmother Hannah, who bears "the perfect semblance of a lily cut, as it were, in shining ebony" (606) upon her breast like the birth mark of every descendant of the royal line.

Despite all her significance, the reader knows very little about Aunt Hannah, the foremother, because she emerges in so few speech situations and interacts with so few people; yet it is her meeting and interaction with the mulatta heroine that is most significant. Aunt Hannah remains the same through the mysticism, the spiritual healings, and the visions, much as Aunt Henny does through the disguise, fraud, and murder. Seemingly insignificant, the foremother is nevertheless persistent and consistent in the literature of early black female writers. She serves major cultural functions by her very presence and through the content and style of her language, not to mention the breadth of knowing that is seldom expressed in conventional ways. According to Alice Childress, the story of the old Negro has not been told. The Negro woman will attain her rightful place in American literature when those of us who care about truth and justice tell her story with full knowledge and appreciation of her (1974, 33).

Black women writers continue the tradition of storytelling through fiction during the Harlem Renaissance. The foremother figure continues to prompt some primary action in the life of the mulatta heroine or principal character while still in her secondary role as foremother in the works of Jessie Redmon Fauset.

NOTES

1. Claudia Tate refers to this meeting more meaningfully as a rescue ("Pauline Hopkins: Our Literary Foremother," 63).

2. Alice Walker argues that "any sexual intercourse between a free man and a human being he owns or controls is rape," thus the appropriateness of the phrase, "raped black mother" ("If the Present Looks Like the Past, What Does the Future Look Like?" 305).

CHAPTER 6

Finding the Foremother in Fauset

The image of the older black woman continues in the Harlem Renaissance in characters who may be minor in the plot but who perform a major service in defining the mulatta heroine or principal female character. In each of Jessie Redmon Fauset's four novels it is possible to establish an indirect or direct link between a foremother figure and the principal female character or mulatta heroine through discourse. As with the works of Jacobs, Harper, and Hopkins, the works of Fauset, published from 1924 to 1933, bring variation yet overall similarity in the correlation between the foremother and principal female character. In *There Is Confusion* (1924) it is possible to establish an indirect link between the older black woman, Mammy, and the principal female character, Joanna Marshall, through the character of Joel Marshall, Mammy's son and Joanna's father. In *The Chinaberry Tree: A Novel of American Life* (1931), Aunt Sal, the mother as foremother, helps to define her daughter and mulatta heroine, Laurentine Strange, and in *Comedy: American Style* (1933) Mrs. Davies influences the life of Teresa Cary, but within the realm of the competing force, Teresa's mother, Olivia. The portrait of Hetty Daniels, in Fauset's *Plum Bun: A Novel Without a Moral* (1928), however, establishes the most definitive correlation between the foremother and the mulatta heroine. Hetty Daniels, the foremother, produces meaningful language that emerges and reemerges as guiding principles in significant episodes of Angela Murray's life.

MAMMY IN *THERE IS CONFUSION*

In Fauset's first novel *There Is Confusion* (1924), Joel Marshall's mother is a former slave and is a Mammy in name only. Ironically, Mammy is the foremother who subverts the stereotypical image of mammy because she resonates a spirit of liberation. Her son Joel inherits this spirit of liberation and reveals it in his expressed desire to achieve greatness. Mammy nurses that desire in Joel, and makes a direct impact on his life; however, the extent to which she indirectly influences Joel's daughter Joanna is most far-reaching.

As a child, Joel frequently sought the resources of the foremother to confirm his desire to be great, for Mammy says, "'As a little tyke, he was always pesterin' me: 'Mammy, I'll be a great man some day, won't I? Mammy, you're gonna help me to be great?'" (9). It is evident that Mammy answered in the affirmative, but it is also evident that she did not realize the generative power of her words. She later recalls, "'How wuz I to know he'd be a great caterer, feedin' bank presidents and everything? Once you know they had him fix a banquet fur President Grant. Sent all the way to Richmond fur 'im. . . . yassuh, my son is sure a great man'" (9). Her language communicates an emotion greater than pride. She communicates her total belief in Joel, and Joel realizes early in life that "his mother knew his ideas and loved them with . . . a fine, albeit somewhat uncomprehending passion and belief " (10).

Thus Joel Marshall has inherited the desire to be great from Mammy, the foremother in the past, and Joanna Marshall also inherits the desire to be great from this foremother through Joel in the present. The language reveals that Mammy, Joel, and Joanna harbor desires for greatness because each uses the same lexical item, "great"; however, the word differs semantically for each character, who represents a different generation. As the social, the cultural, and the political climates change, so do the word, the concept, and the language in general change over time. In telling a listener about her son's childhood desire and young adult success, Mammy shares her pride in his material success so that her perception of his success becomes communal: "As a little tyke, his mother used to tell her friends, 'he was always pesterin me'" (9). Joel possesses a deep desire to be great through education and leadership, honestly and faithfully, which indicates if not the involvement of others then certainly a regard for others, for the narrator confirms, "This was no selfish wish" (10). Mammy engages the community and Joel regards others. Joanna, who never interacts with the foremother directly but benefits indirectly from the influence of her language, is initially absorbed with individual success and according to McDowell is a "stubbornly independent careerist" (1987, 98). Joanna thus distorts the cultural and communal wisdom of the foremother. Later, however, she comes to see her performances in black churches as her favorites and sees herself in New York as a pioneer for the race in stage productions.

Drawing from a singular source directly and indirectly, Joel's and Joanna's similar desires are mirrored in the similar events that occur in their lives. The origin of their similar desires can be linked to the influence of the foremother, Mammy, who recalls that Joel expressed the desire to be great just after the Civil War. She notes that when Joel pestered her about his desire to be great, "'it was a long time ago, just a year or so after the war'" (9). Her recollection of temporal events is telling. If Joel expresses the desire to be great a year or two after the War, one can infer that his young life during slavery was not shrouded with doubt and fear, but instilled with confidence and fearlessness. "At night the little boy picked out the stories of Napoleon, Lincoln, and Garrison, all white men, it is true; but Lincoln had been poor and Napoleon unknown and yet they had risen to the highest possible state" (10). Joel's seeing the white male as his hero as a very young boy is further indication that Mammy either guarded him from the harsh realities of slavery or that Mammy did not experience the harsh realities of slavery. In fact, Mammy's language, in general, does not bemoan the injustices of slavery. She shares no incidents of injustice in her own life or in the life of her fellow slaves during her brief appearance in the novel. Even the narrator barely touches on the injustice of slavery when Joel thinks about those forces that were against him:

> His color, his poverty, meant nothing to his ardent heart; those were nature's limitations, placed deliberately about one, he could see dimly, to try one's strength on. *But that he should have a father broken and sickened by slavery who lingered on and on!* That after that father's death the little house should burn down! (10 emphasis added).

The voices of neither the foremother, her son, nor the narrator blame slavery with vehemence. The narrator merely indicates that Joel resented his father's illness because it lingered, not because his father was broken and sickened by slavery. Perhaps Fauset should be criticized for presenting such a calm recollection of slavery from the perspective of the enslaved, or perhaps the name "Mammy" itself suggests the compromise that surrounds the figure of this older black woman. Nevertheless, to instill confidence and self-assurance during enslavement indicates that Mammy was politically enslaved but mentally liberated during slavery, because Joel obviously possessed the spirit of liberation as a youngster and the text provides evidence that he passed it on as an adult. At the age of five Joanna demands of Joel what Joel demanded of Mammy. Joanna demands that Joel tell her a story about somebody great—"'I want to hear about a man who did things nobody else could do'" (13). Her male perception of greatness parallels Joel's expressed desire to be a "man among men" (10). With the same assurance that his mother communicated, Joel tells Joanna that "'nothing in reason is impossible'" (18). He attaches no gender to his assessment of attainment. Joanna thus believes that she will sing in Carnegie Hall. When her friend Peter responds, "'colored people don't get any chance at that kind of thing,'" Joanna retorts, "'Colored people can do everything that anybody else can do. They've already done it'" (45). The narrator credits Joanna's response to her extensive reading, yet it was Joel who initiated her reading program during early childhood because of her inquisitiveness about greatness (13). Joanna's response to Peter shows that she envisions no limits in a world of possibilities. This confidence and assurance point back to Mammy's unstated affirmation of Joel's expressed desire to be great. Mammy nursed Joel's desire to be great despite the contrary instincts implicit in enslavement. Similarly, Joel nurses Joanna's desire to be great even though he had to forego his own desire to be a "man among men."

Like her father, Joanna uses her ingenuity to get what she wants. Joel's ingenuity was born out of the necessity to remain close to his ailing mother and to earn income. He started a small business by opening a sandwich stand adjacent to his home. Joel used his ingenuity again when he seized a fleeting moment of popularity after it became known that he prepared a meal for President Grant. He capitalized on the opportunity and moved his business and his mother from Richmond to New York (11). Joanna uses her ingenuity to resist racism when she persuades the great French dance instructor to hold a separate class for dancers of color (96). She also uses her ingenuity when she adapts her professional dance routine to a children's dance routine rooted in the African American culture. Joanna uses her culture as a resource to make her first major step toward greatness. Joanna's talent draws applause even from a conservative board and a conservative audience (229). As Asante points out, one need not leave the source of power in order to be universal. True universalism occurs when an artist captures the special story of his or her own culture in ways that make an impact on others (1992, 20).

Mammy gauged the success of Joel's catering business by the impact it made on others. Mammy saw Joel as a great businessman because he gained regional popularity. When Mammy claimed Joel's greatness she challenged a society that erects actual economic obstacles to black success in general and the constraints of public opinion toward the black male in particular because she undercut the lazy, comic negro stereotype. Because of Mammy, Joel embraced the idea as a youngster that he was exceptional and envisioned that he would hold a position in the future that would place him in the public eye and garner the applause of the masses: "The kind of greatness he had envisaged had been that which gets one before the public eye, which makes one a leader of causes, a 'man among men'" (10). It is evident that Joanna, in turn, is greatly concerned about public opinion because she is class conscious and admonishes those around her to associate with those who are class conscious and to act according to the standards prescribed by that class. For instance, Joanna perceives that the lower class enjoys the atmosphere of the cabaret and the middle class enjoys the atmosphere of live theatre (159), and, most importantly, that the two classes of people are mutually exclusive. Similarly Joanna views her sister's sewing and Maggie's sewing as two divergent activities. Her sister sews when she is inspired, whereas the text implies that Maggie sews when she is in need of extra income. The former is creative artistic expression and the latter is mere work (78). Her class bias is most clearly expressed in her intervention to prevent her brother's marriage to Maggie. Only gradually will she relent in her class bias and discover the value of community implicit in Joel's and Mammy's attitudes.

Despite her intervention in the lives of others, Joanna is relentless in her dreams of success, for "Joanna was really sick at heart to think that her beautiful dreams of success for both of them [her and Peter] might not be realized" (162), whereas her father Joel had to stifle his dreams (11). Joel's plans for formal schooling at a seminary were thwarted; nevertheless, his business skills were sharpened. It is as though his longing for greatness actually produced great things, for Joel transmitted to his namesake not only his desires, but Mammy's nurturance that fueled his desires: "she was like a little living echo out of his forgotten past" (9). Joanna, who "was so completely like himself" posed the question, "'Daddy, you'll help me to be a great woman, somebody you'll be proud of?'" (14). Joel's unstated affirmative response, like Mammy's, is evident from the events that unfold in Joanna's life. Joanna's priority is to be a great woman. When she is older she places her relationship with Peter second to her career ambitions (McDowell "Neglected Dimension . . . " 94) similarly to Joel, who married only after his catering business became successful and his mother died. Joanna's wish for success in the theatre exemplifies the same desire for applause from the masses as had motivated her father, who had desired to be a minister, "a man with a great name and a healing tongue" (10). A final way in which Joel's desires shape his life and are reflected in Joanna's life is that Joel attains economic success instead of greatness as a "man among men," and Joanna ultimately attains success in marriage instead of greatness as a professional singer and dancer in the theater. Like the contrary instincts implicit in Mammy's life during enslavement, the contrary constraints of preferential treatment and lack of access operate in Joanna's life. Whereas Mammy battled contrary instincts to sustain life when she labored in someone else's kitchen, Joanne battles contrary instincts in her attempt to construct a pathway to success and ultimately greatness in the performing arts when she arranges separate professional dance instruction for dancers of color.

The desire for greatness originates from the foremother, Mammy, and makes a direct impact on Joel Marshall's life and an indirect impact on Joanna's life through Joel. The far-reaching impact on Joanna's life is that her desire for greatness initially evolves into an aggressive competition and an unhealthy disregard for others. Joel, under the direct influence of the foremother, "wanted to do honestly and faithfully the things that bring greatness" (10). When Joanna shares with her sister her fear of losing Peter, the narrator says, "another girl in Joanna's place might not have suffered so intensely. But Joanna, poor creature, was doomed by her very virtues. That same singlemindedness which had made her so engrossed in her art, now proved her undoing" (176). Peter gives a similar depiction of Joanna: "'I tell you what, Maggie, Joanna's got no heart, she's all head, all ideas and if you don't see and act her way, she's got no use for you'" (169). Even though he misses those softer feelings that Joanna represses or delays expressing, his observation is partly true. But Joanna moves from her initial single-minded, individual ambition and urgent need to prove that blacks are capable and talented people to an eventual recognition that success is communal and inclusive rather than individual and exclusive. Without realizing the full significance of her decisions and actions, Joanna actually engages in a level of success which parallels the communal and inclusive vision of success revealed in the language of the foremother. It is not only Joanna's willingness to share her talent and to serve as director of music for a colored school (222) that exemplify elements of the communal and inclusive, but that she is actually inspired when she sings before black church congregations. Evidence of her willing service and inspiration balance the competing dominant visions of the exceptional and the extreme in success and greatness, respectively. Success and greatness, regardless of their semantic changes over time, are dependent upon respect for family and community, and support of and by the community.

AUNT SAL IN *THE CHINABERRY TREE*

In Fauset's third novel, *The Chinaberry Tree: A Novel of American Life* (1931), the foremother plays a much larger role than Mammy in *There Is Confusion*. Aunt Sal plays the roles of both foremother and biological mother to Laurentine Strange, the mulatta heroine. Aunt Sal redefines the foremother's role, for she loves the figure that represents oppression for her and her people—the figure that constructs those images which she should oppose, undermine, and destroy. She loves the powerful white male and father of her child, Colonel Frank Halloway, despite the tension it causes in the community and within her family. Aunt Sal continues to love Colonel Halloway even after his death because her house, land, and a portion of his legal will remind Aunt Sal and the community of Colonel Halloway's reciprocal love for her despite his white wife, white children, white extended family, and friends. Even many years later, Aunt Sal "felt free to think of her dead lover—with ease and gratefulness and complete acceptance" (340).

Reflecting briefly on black women's works covered thus far, no writer portrays the foremother figure as expressing love and commitment for the white father of her child. In fact, the only previously discussed foremother who is clearly a "raped black mother" is Aunt Hannah in Hopkins's *Of One Blood*, although the language surrounding Jacobs's Aunt Nancy also strongly suggests this abuse. No other foremother's possible intimate relations with white males are revealed. In early white female works included in this study, the reader finds fondness and loyalty, but no intimacy, and in the one case of a foremother who was a sexual partner with a white master, the woman expressed no love or attachment for him. Aunt Sal, then, exemplifies the complexity, the distinction, and the conflict that the foremother figure embodies because neither the foremother nor her circumstances remain static. She is a figure rich in variations, suited to the fundamental urge to realism in black women writers.

Christian observes that although Aunt Sal might have been a woman of passion, her mulatta daughter, Laurentine, is a lady, except for her manner of birth and the strained strangeness that seem to come from her mixed blood (Christian 1980, 44). Whereas Aunt Sal celebrates happiness regardless of the source (10), Laurentine prays for "peace, security, a name, and a home life like other women" (21). What Aunt Sal possesses transcends happiness and reaches the depths of joy, because she is able to resist the dictates of society and the community. She perceives her experience as a special kind of happiness which many other people would have mistaken for suffering, pain, and disgrace (168). Even though Aunt Sal is happy with the memory of her white lover, she never fails to empathize with Laurentine, who seeks the constraints of conformity. Laurentine was "almost ridiculously careful of her name and fame. In brief, she was the epitome of all those virtues and restraints which colored men so arrogantly demand in the women they make their wives" (124). Laurentine prays, "'Oh God, you know all I want is a chance to show them how decent I am'" (36). Laurentine internalizes the community's view that her mixed heritage resulted in bad blood. Laurentine is initially defined by the foremother in that what Aunt Sal represents, Laurentine strives not to represent, not out of hate for her mother but out of the need to conform to the dictates of the community and the society. Laurentine prays that she will be like other women, hence not so much unlike Aunt Sal but unlike the community's view of Aunt Sal. Aunt Sal recognizes the differences between herself and Laurentine: "She wanted Laurentine to be happy in the safe, normal way which she craved, because safe and normal ways were the only ways Laurentine understood. 'She couldn't be happy in my way or Frank's,' her mother thought still smiling to herself " (168). Laurentine, on the other hand, feels pity for her mother: "She was sorry for her mother. She knew that her mother took upon herself the blame for everything" (61). Aunt Sal attempts to undo for Laurentine what her reputation has done when she attempts to appeal to Laurentine's male acquaintance, Phil Hackett, to maintain his friendship with her daughter. After her failure, Aunt Sal explains to Laurentine with frustration: "'I thought if I went to him as a mother—oh Laurentine, if I could only have been your father too!'" (67) Aunt Sal expresses regret only insofar as her reputation makes a direct negative impact on Laurentine's personal relationships. She attempts action in a one-on-one battle for Laurentine, but she wages no war against the community. Aunt Sal can only help Laurentine in her sincere desire for Laurentine's happiness. She cannot teach by example because Aunt Sal adheres to the precepts of her heart to survive.

As expected of the foremother, Aunt Sal's exceptional nature is portrayed not only in her relationship with the mulatta heroine through discourse, but through the response of minor characters. Melissa, Aunt Sal's niece, observes that "life held no further fears, seeing she [Aunt Sal] had met them and left them behind her" (186). Melissa, better able to appreciate Aunt Sal than Laurentine is, formulates her perception of Aunt Sal's past as though it is a mark of achievement. Mr. Stede, the gardener, believes Aunt Sal to be "an absolutely right person, a law unto herself" (233). Aunt Sal defines her values for herself regardless of the constraints implicit in public opinion. It is Laurentine's fiance, Dr. Denleigh, who finally helps Laurentine put her mother's past in perspective. Dr. Denleigh views the past relationship between Aunt Sal and Colonel Halloway as "awe-inspiring" because they permitted love to prevail despite social constraints (160). The result for Laurentine is that "the old familiar burden was loosening; someday it would disappear" (160-61). Dr. Denleigh's concern about Laurentine's self-perception addresses Laurentine's fetish about possessing bad blood because of her mixed heritage, but he provides no successful psychological cure. Reconciliation with Aunt Sal is a psychological process that begins and continues, but it never ends for Laurentine.

As she redefines the figure of foremother, Aunt Sal defines negatively, by contrast, the emotional and behavioral traits of the mulatta heroine in that Aunt Sal provides a personal relationship model that instills in Laurentine a determination to strive to conform to the conventions of the community and society. As in *There is Confusion*, the novel ends with a measure of hope for Laurentine's growth in receptivity of the foremother's values in that she possesses a heightened awareness for the emotional needs of others. Where she was once unfeeling, Laurentine now genuinely empathizes with the emotional plight of her cousin, Melissa, who was unknowingly engaged to her brother, Malory. This change is revealed in Melissa's response to

Laurentine's empathy: "'You mean you don't hate me any more'? . . . She didn't remember ever having seen Laurentine cry before, either" (334). Laurentine's empathy approaches Aunt Sal's heartfelt desire for Laurentine's happiness and normalcy in life.

MRS. DAVIES IN *COMEDY: AMERICAN STYLE*

In Fauset's fourth novel, *Comedy: American Style* (1933), Mrs. Davies, the foremother, is a more familiar image than the reticent fair-skinned Aunt Sal in *The Chinaberry Tree*. The foremother, Mrs. Davies, is a large, dark woman with a wide, jolly smile. She influences the young Teresa Cary through her words and touch. It is Mrs. Davies's expressive language and expression through touch that draw others to her.

Jacquelyn McLendon observes that "Mrs. Davies physically represents the stereotypical ideal mother, yet her image is problematic because it conjures a vision of 'mammy' or 'aunty,' and it is subversive in its sharp contrast to the image of the colorist Olivia (1995, 60). Yet her real and simple human warmth seems to transcend stereotype, and her opposition to Olivia's loyalty to whiteness distinguishes her from the loyal mammy. Mrs. Davies creates an atmosphere in her home that is an extension of herself—happiness, warmth, and comfort (McLendon 1995, 59). It is the atmosphere that Mrs. Davies creates, the appearance that she possesses, the touch that she shares, and the word that she speaks that define this memorable and affective foremother. For example, Mrs. Davies says repeatedly to Teresa and her peers, "'I want you all to be happy.'" The narrator describes the foremother as "exhaling such a sense of comfort" that "Teresa would cross over to the billowy dark woman . . . and slip her little hand into hers" (44). On another occasion:

> Teresa gravitates toward her and, as usual, receives a word and a slight caress. For a fleeting moment Mrs. Davies puts a warm arm about her. "You look a little peaked, Honey. Eat a lot of them sandwiches and join in and sing and dance with the rest of them. Don't let yourself be too quiet, you're only young once, you know." The homely, kindly words lit a glow about the child's chilled, apprehensive heart (48).

While she basks in the nurturing radiance of Mrs. Davies's personage, Teresa is able to guard against her mother Olivia's obsession with whiteness.

Olivia cherishes whiteness as the ideal and makes every effort to win each member of her family to her way of thinking. As a result, Olivia causes the death of her youngest son, who is dark in complexion, and reaps emotional despair in her husband and daughter. Teresa admits that "'I haven't got the stuff in me to disobey her'" (55); yet she is drawn to Mrs. Davies, who intensifies her warm words and touch and "put[s] her warm arms about her [and says] 'you were always my girl, Teresa. Be happy, Honey!'" (61) Olivia, on the other hand, communicates to Teresa that to be happy means "don't be colored" (83). McLendon also notes the tension that exists throughout the text because of these two competing forces. She says that "Mrs. Davies represents ideal motherhood, but Olivia represents the dominant maternal voice in the text" (1995, 65). The language of the foremother is like a balm. Her words nurture, praise, and encourage, whereas Olivia's language is like a weapon. It shatters, exposes, and hurts. Thus the two produce conflict in language use and tension in the text, only to provide further evidence that Mrs. Davies, not Olivia, is the true foremother!

Teresa vows that she will be a mother like Mrs. Davies: "She would grow up and have four children. All of them should be like her little brother Oliver and she would be a mother like Mrs. Davies" (48). For a time she actually plays the role of mother for her beautiful, brown younger brother, whom Olivia would not love because of his obvious color. In Teresa's absence, Oliver, too, seeks the nurturing atmosphere of Mrs. Davies's home, the source of Teresa's warmth and responsiveness. On one of his visits with Mrs. Davies and her daughter Marise, Mrs. Davies "affectionately shood him home" but in doing so again intensifies her words with a touch by giving him "a motherly hug and kiss" and saying, "'and mind you stay happy.'" Mrs. Davies communicates a sense of well-being to both mind and body. Leaving her nurturing environment, "Oliver went off in the thin tingling November rain, loving them both for their sweet tactfulness" (203).

Thadious Davis notes in the Introduction to *Comedy: American Style* that Marise Davies is an undisputed leader among the youth and possesses a strong sense of self (1995, xxvii); however, the critic does not attribute the source of Marise's strength. Clearly it is Mrs. Davies's influence and her culinary skills that shape Marise's character and that bloom as professional dance skills in her daughter. Of course, it is Marise's name, not Mrs. Davies's, that is reflected in the neon lights. Alice Walker speaks of a similar mother who sings or weaves, but whose daughter's name is signed to some other form of art such as poetry (1983b, 243). The daughter's name and poem the world will see and know; the invisible source—the foremother—remains unknown.

The foremother is a known source of power which can be illuminated through the language. Marise matures but does not move completely away from her mother, the source of power, while Teresa matures and is moved forcibly away. Marise maintains contact while she meets the challenges of her career as a successful professional dancer and as she engages in the challenges of marriage. Teresa obviously admires Marise for her determination and optimism: "'If I were just someone like Marise'" (55). As long as Teresa maintains some form of contact with Mrs. Davies, she too benefits greatly from her foremotherly sustenance, but only during her childhood. When Olivia sends Teresa away to school and later contrives to keep her in Europe, Teresa becomes "silent, pale, subdued, the ghost of her former self. . . ." During the last two years she had more than once contemplated suicide (324-25). Thus, out of the range of Mrs. Davies's powerful words, "Be happy," and her laying on of hands, Teresa clearly loses the sources which are vital to her growth and well-being, and accelerates in an emotional, downward spiral. Thus Marise, as a minor character, lives out the long-term influence of the foremother.

HETTY DANIELS IN *PLUM BUN*

Jessie Redmon Fauset's works reveal varied responses to the complex nature of the foremother through the figure of the mulatta heroine or principal character. Thus far Joanna enacts a one-sided and excessive version of the foremother's perception of success, Laurentine resists the lesson that can be learned from a non-conformist foremother, and Teresa is forcibly removed from the power of the word and the healing touch of the foremother. Each is essentially removed from the situational context of the foremother because of death, resistance, or separation. While neither the heroine nor the foremother in each case is perfect, each foremother is correct in what she is willing to offer the heroine from her cultural knowledge and life experience. Fauset's second and most popular novel, *Plum Bun: A Novel Without a Moral* (1928) also portrays the less than perfect foremother who nevertheless communicates to the mulatta heroine the concept of perfection in the virtuous woman.

Hetty Daniels, the foremother in *Plum Bun*, advances from Saturday maid to live-in housekeeper, companion, and chaperone after the death of Mr. and Mrs. Murray (65). Hetty also serves as a model for the artist and mulatta heroine, Angela Murray. Angela "would begin sketching, usually ending up with a new view of Hetty Daniels's head" (65). Hetty's head serves not only as a literal model but also as a figurative one. Figuratively, Hetty's thoughts act as gatekeepers of Victorian principles. Regardless of the literal angle or tilt that the artist, Angela, demands of the model, Hetty adheres to the principles that direct her life and maintain her unchanging world view.

Hetty believes that models are chosen for their beauty and not some other artistic quality (65). Hetty sees herself as beautiful because she upholds the principles of a virtuous woman. Central to the foremother-mulatta heroine relationship in *Plum Bun* is the language that Hetty shares with Angela during one of her Sunday afternoon sittings:

> Miss Daniels' great fetish was sexual morality. "Then young fellers was always 'round me thick ez bees; wasn't any night they wasn't more fellows in my kitchen then you an' Jinny ever has in yore parlour. But I never listened to none of the' talk, jist held out agin 'em and kept my pearl of great price untarnished. I aimed then and I'm continual to aim to be a verjous woman."

> Her unslaked yearnings gleamed suddenly out of her eyes, transforming her usually rather expressionless face into something wild and avid. The dark brown immobile mask of her skin made an excellent foil for the vividness of an emotion which was so apparent, so palpable that it seemed like something superimposed upon the background of her countenance (66).

As McLendon points out, the narrator's description reveals the unnaturalness of Hetty's having to suppress her sexual desires (1995, 38). Angela penetratingly views her artistic rendering of Hetty's face as expressing unfulfilled desire, whereas a fellow white art student views it as expressing the unhappiness stereotypically expected to be associated with any member of the colored race (70). Both views reflect a state of unnaturalness in Hetty, the white student's because it reflects a generalization of the black race, and Angela's because at this time of her life delayed gratification (for freedom, power, and material things) creates discomfort and thus should be avoided.

Hetty not only reflects an image of unnaturalness but irony in characterization. It is ironic that the figure of the single, black, virtuous female, Hetty Daniels, subverts the stereotypical wench image associated with the black female, while Angela's friend, the single, white female, Paulette Lister, supports the sexually promiscuous image not usually associated with the white female. McLendon observes that "Fauset displaces the alleged sexual promiscuity of black women onto the bodies of white women" (1995, 37). For example, Angela's response to Paulette Lister's conversation about male-female relationships parallels Hetty's sentiments: "'An affair'? gasped Angela. . . . 'A lover?'. . . . 'And you've no intention of marrying?'" (106). Even though promiscuity will eventually play a role in Angela's masquerading as a white female, at this point in her new role, Angela reaches back to her community as a resource. The community that she has escaped Angela now draws on in order to select a standard by which to measure others: "Beyond question some of the coloured people of her acquaintance must have lived in a manner which would not bear inspection, but she could not think of one who would thus have discussed it calmly with either friend or stranger" (107). Angela views Hetty as the extreme in her pronouncement of how she keeps her "pearl of great price untarnished." Such a pronouncement could communicate in general the conduct expected of a virtuous woman. One expects such allusions and implicit language when one broaches such intimate topics, unlike Paulette's glaring revelations, "'Why yes, a lover. I've had . . . I've had more than one'" (106).

Angela interprets the semantic level of Paulette's words with difficulty, just as she experiences difficulty with the semantic import of Roger's words later. Implicit in the text is that Angela is more in tune with the visual, than the verbal. Angela's artistic "specialty lay along the line of reproducing, of interpreting on a face the emotion which lay back of that expression" (111) as Angela does with Hetty. Angela is confident in her talent for interpreting the visual over the verbal, and the countenance over the discourse. For example, of the Fourteenth Street types Angela "depict[s] . . . the countenance of a purse-proud but lonely man, of the silken inanity of a society girl, of the smiling despair of a harlot. Even in her own mind she hesitated before the use of the terrible word, but association was teaching her to call a spade a spade"

(111). Angela is perceptive of most types, but what of the rich and powerful white male? Angela misinterprets the countenance and discourse of Roger despite Hetty's explicit, instructive discourse regarding her own past male admirers. Angela mistakenly "was sure now that he loved and would marry her, for it never occurred to her that men bestowed attentions such as these on a passing fancy" (130). It is the competing forces of warring ideals that blur Angela's vision.

Paulette Lister and Hetty Daniels function as competing forces in Angela's life as she struggles with the issue of passing in New York and its requirement of severing ties in Philadelphia. She wavers between the new and the familiar. In contrast to Paulette's expressed defiance, "'I don't care what people think'" (112) is Hetty's articulated stance on maintaining her virtue, and that value system with which Angela is most familiar. Even the narrator indicates parallel roles of Paulette and Hetty in saying that Angela is "playing a game now, a game against public tradition on the one hand and family instinct on the other" (146). Paulette represents public tradition and Hetty represents family instinct. Yet as Angela observes Paulette's countenance as Paulette talks about desire ("Her face for a moment was all desire. Beautiful but terrible too"), she thinks, "'She actually looks like Hetty Daniels.'" Perhaps a hidden similarity between the two resides in Hetty's repressed sexuality. But upon further consideration of Paulette's countenance, she concludes that "there was no longer any beauty in Hetty's face" (126-27). In Hetty's face Angela sees "something wild and avid" (66). Regardless of Angela's artistic rendition, as the foremother Hetty holds a definition of beauty that eludes the artist and the canvas because beauty radiates from pride—the excessive pride of being a virtuous woman. As an artist, Angela captures Hetty's repressed sexual desire but does not capture on canvas Hetty's perception of beauty. The emotion of repressed sexual desire thus overshadows the perception of outer beauty associated with the image of the virtuous woman.

To remain within the realm of the definition of a virtuous woman is central to Angela's struggle. Angela rationalizes Roger's inappropriate behavior when she confesses to her sister Virginia, "'I think his ultimate intentions are all right'" (166). Her language contradicts Hetty's recollection about the behavior of her young male friends and her response to their advances; Hetty in her wisdom "never listened" and thus was not tempted to rationalize inappropriate behavior. Angela rationalizes inappropriate behavior in a weak attempt to adhere to virtuousness. The virtuous woman, however, is the ideal and thus unattainable in spirit for both the foremother and the heroine. Angela's rationalizing is apparent when Virginia asks, "'Isn't he a white man? Well, what kind of intentions would he have toward a coloured woman?'" Angela confesses, "'He doesn't know I'm coloured. And besides some of them [white men] are decent'" (166). Angela's rationalizing of inappropriate behavior and passing for white pose as disguises similar to the foremother's self-righteous modeling of the virtuous woman, despite her desire.

Despite the foremother's flaws, however, she remains a significant moral touchstone for the mulatta heroine. Angela frequently recalls past experiences and the words of the foremother during her months of estrangement from family and friends just as she recalls the words of her deceased mother. She remembers Hetty's pronouncement: "'He who would have friends must show himself friendly'" (168). Since she has chosen to pass, Angela regrets that she has neglected to maintain correspondence with her sister. Her deceased mother, Mattie Murray, was a good mother who expressed the desire that Angela be a great artist someday (55). She was a good mother even though she transposed the serious act of passing into a Saturday afternoon game activity. Because of the negative influence from her mother, Angela transposes this Saturday afternoon game activity of passing into a daily serious act of passing. Angela later determines that color is of little importance and companionship is of great importance. It is at times like these that Angela recalls her mother's words: "'You get so taken up with the problem of living, with just life itself, that by and by being coloured or not is just one thing more or less that you have to contend with'" (251-52). Both Hetty's and Mrs. Murray's words are instructive, but it is Hetty's commentary about virtue that reemerges consistently throughout the novel to further define and develop the artistic character of Angela Murray.

In her artistic rendition of Hetty's head, Angela selects descriptors such as "expressionless," "immobile mask," and "dark brown" to depict her varying perspectives of Hetty's facial features. When it is the artist herself who elicits a telling response from the male perspective, descriptors are meaningful in a different way:

> She was still bruised in spirit that she had taken it upon herself to go
> to Anthony's room. But now that it seemed to avail nothing it loomed
> up before her in all its social significance. She was that creature

whom men, in their selfish fear, have contrived to paint as the least
attractive of human kind—"a girl who runs after men" (296).

As Angela constructs artistic images of varied types, men construct
social images of female types. Men master the art of social
significance—men construct the images and define the images
according to their own perspectives—in their selfish fear of losing
control of the construction and the definition. Barbara Ewell argues that
in a patriarchal society women are defined as self-less. They are named
and described only in terms of their relationship to men—daughter,
wife, mother, sister, widow. More specifically they are described in
their sexual relationship to men—virgin, whore, mistress, spinster
(1992, 158). Fittingly, Roger expresses to Angela later that "'not every
man is capable of appreciating a woman who breaks through the
conventions for him. Some men mistake it for cheapness but others see
it for what it is and love more deeply and gratefully'" (196). The
conventions are erected by men; therefore, they manipulate facets of the
conventions at will. Roger insinuates that he would appreciate Angela's
being unconventional. Angela's pride binds her discourse of
interrogation when she cannot ask Roger, "But why shouldn't we
marry?" (196), whereas Hetty's pride releases her discourse of
confirmation that "'I aimed then and I'm continual to aim to be a
verjous woman'" (66). Hetty clings to the conventions of the virtuous
woman, even though she is wild with desire.

Angela's own sexual desires and Roger's advances produce "this
crisis in her life which so frightened and attracted her. She was the
more frightened because she felt that attraction" (169). The attraction
alluded to here recalls the expressions on Paulette's and Hetty's faces:
"all desire" (126), and "wild and avid" (66) respectively. Like Hetty,
Angela initially possesses pride and self-confidence: "If she did not
withdraw from her acquaintanceship with Roger now, even though she
committed no overt act she would never be the same; she could never
again face herself with the old, unshaken pride and self-confidence"
(177). Hetty had said with pride that she "kept [her] pearl of great price
untarnished" (66). Angela attempts to play the game of love but proves
to be an amateur, for she wavers in the face of Roger's proposition,
"'I'm asking you to live in my house, to live for me; to be my girl.'"
(182). Angela questions, "should she strike him. . . . or should she stay
and hear it out?" (182) Unlike Hetty, Angela "hated herself for staying
and listening" (183). Hetty "never listened to none of the talk" (66).

Roger wishes to impress his listening audience of one when he includes in his game strategy a search through the annals of history to prove the authenticity of his proposal. He argues that "'some of the sweetest unions in history have been of this kind'" (184). Angela draws on her knowledge of her experiences in the recent past when she looks again to her family and community for answers. She argues that "'relationships of the kind you describe don't exist among the people I know'" (184). She is thinking of her parents and her neighbors, the Hallowells, and the Hensons, whose lives were indeed like "open books" (184). Angela does not include Hetty here because her parents and neighbors represent what Ann duCille calls the "coupling convention" in which Hetty does not participate. Hetty's life is also, however, an open book. The significance of this community is evident throughout the novel, because Angela repeatedly draws on that with which she is most familiar—the words of Hetty and her mother, and the presence of her sister—"her own flesh and blood, one of her own people" (189) to help her in her struggle to make the right decision. Yet, "all her little world, judging it by the standards by which she was used to measuring people, was tumbling in ruins at her feet" (193) because she listens to Roger. Angela hears Roger's voice breaking, pleading, promising (203) and finally gives in to him, whereas Hetty, bound by convention, "never listened to none of the talk, jist held out agin 'em" (66).

Even though Hetty is flawed in her modeling morality, and Angela is flawed in her exercising freedom, Hetty's influence in defining Angela emerges yet again when Angela reminisces about her past after submitting to Roger's wishes and believing that she was experiencing happiness (204). She includes Hetty Daniels in her remembrance along with the neighbors and friends whom she has left in her hometown of Philadelphia. It is actually Hetty whom she foregrounds over and above the others:

> The Hensons, the Hallowells, Hetty Daniels,—Jinny! . . . . Before her rose the eager, starved face of Hetty Daniels; now she herself was cognizant of phases of life for which Hetty longed but so condemned. Angela could imagine the envy back of the tone in which Hetty, had she but known it, would have expressed her disapproval of her former charge's manner of living. "Mattie Murray's girl, Angela, had gone straight to the bad; she's living a life of sin with some man in New

York." . . . And then the final, blasting indictment. "He's a white
man, too. Can you beat that?" (205)

She clearly judges herself through Hetty's eyes, having internalized
Hetty's and her family's values long before, during her impressionable
youth. Angela does come to terms with her decisions and actions over
time, understanding the values underlying the rigid behavioral code
represented by Hetty:

> And she began to see the conventions, the rules that govern life, in a
> new light; she realized suddenly that for all their granite-like coldness
> and precision they also represented fundamental facts; a sort of
> concentrated compendium of the art of living and therefore as much
> to be observed and respected as warm, vital impulses (228).

Hetty, then, is the model for "the art of living" because she, like the
artist's finished representation, is fixed in a monumental form that
represents the unchanging figure of the virtuous woman. Because Hetty
is fixed and unyielding in her representation of the virtuous woman she
is portrayed as a thing beyond the dynamism of humanity. Hetty, the
foremother, then, is the monument, the model, and the law to which the
mulatta heroine constantly refers for guidance, but at the same time the
mulatta heroine struggles with her own personal proclivities, cultural
conflicts, and natural desires. Unrealistically, Angela "dreamed that she
alone of all people in the world was exempt from ordinary law" (232).
Hetty kept the letter, if not the spirit, of the law. Angela learns to
respect the standards and conventions, but she also learns that the
impossible ideals ring false in real life experiences because of their
rigidity. Angela recognizes the wisdom reflected in some of these
conventions even though Hetty carries them to extremes. If Angela had
followed Hetty's example in her naivete, after all, she might not have
been taken in by Roger's promises of stability and would have realized
that a situation that encouraged cutting family ties and that relied on a
lie (passing) was inherently false. On the other hand, she was
compelled to learn from her own experience how to balance the
gratification of desire rampantly encouraged in her generation by the
age and New York environment with the long-term stability of family
and cultural values. Angela finally uses the foremother's wisdom when
she states publicly that she is a member of the black race. Her words,

like Hetty's tells of what and who she truly wishes to be, as she now strives for a more culturally conscious level of freedom.

The foremotherly wisdom inscribed in Fauset's works varies in complexity and in its definition of the mulatta heroine or principal female character. McDowell observes that Fauset establishes images of black life and culture and portrays women and blacks with more complexity and authenticity than was popular for the time (1985, 100). The portrait of the foremother varies in amount and depth of dialogue. Her proximity to the mulatta heroine or principal female character varies with each text, and she garners numerous to no responses from minor characters. Although the foremother remains on the periphery, a connection between her and the mulatta heroine exists in the discourse. The connection to the past must be cherished at any level. Bell hooks exemplifies the events of Angela Murray's life when she says that "maintaining contact is ongoing acknowledgement of the primacy of one's past, affirming the reality that such bonds are not severed just because one enters a new environment or moves toward a different class" (80). Fauset obviously supports the significance of maintaining a connection to one's past because in each novel she portrays a character who represents the past for the principal character. Elements of the past emerge in the present in the forms of incentive, deterrence, nurturance, and idealism. To acknowledge the connection between the older black woman and the mulatta heroine is to subvert the stereotypical mammy image portrayed in early white women's literature and to re-envision the presumed stereotypical mammy image in early black female literature. In support of this study is McLendon's claim that Hetty Daniels revises rather than parallels black female characters in antebellum novels. She also observes that Fauset does not depict dark, uneducated folk as hopeless (1995, 39). It is repeated throughout this investigation that the foremother possesses cultural wisdom rather than the formal education of the dominant culture. In her wisdom she propagates established codes of morality, as Hetty does in *Plum Bun,* or establishes her own codes of morality, as Aunt Sal does in *The Chinaberry Tree*. The foremother politicizes her own personal desires by using dialogue to instill them into others, as Mammy nurtures greatness in *There Is Confusion* and Mrs. Davies commands happiness in *Comedy: American Style.*

The foremother continues to perform major functions in the works of black women writers even in her secondary role in the plots and in her minimal discourse in the speech situations. As this study concludes by glancing at recent works, specific factors in the evolution of the foremother emerging in the works of Zora Neale Hurston, Ann Petry, and Gloria Naylor further illuminate the subversion of the stereotypical mammy in early white women's fiction and the consistent presence of the complex foremother figure in early and later black women's fiction.

CHAPTER 7

Conclusion: The Legacy of the Foremother

The foremother figure portrayed in early black women's literature revises the stereotypical mammy figure. Many early white women writers inscribe and depict the superior-inferior hierarchy in narrative and character dialogue. Regardless of the degree to which the white female measures up to the myth of the ideal white lady (e.g., Marie St. Clair, *Uncle Tom's Cabin*), she is portrayed to be superior to the older black woman and stereotypical mammy, whose very existence is generally defined by loyalty, work, and responsibility in these texts.

The process of re-vision moves the older black woman figure beyond the confines of loyalty, work, and responsibility. As the foremother, the older black woman is not confined by definition; instead her humanity is illuminated by redefinition. She is simple not so much because of stereotyping, but because of limited formal education and basic unchanging values. She has a new complexity because of her spirituality and other-worldliness. Although her physical portrait is vague in the works of minor nineteenth-century writers, she becomes increasingly well-defined in the works of major black women writers. She speaks words of wisdom that are dynamic in their impact on the mulatta heroine. Her words convey meaning that is varied, combining human experience with nature and the physical with the spiritual realm. Over time, the foremothers themselves are increasingly and realistically varied and sometimes flawed. Finally, in this illumination by redefinition the foremother, despite her secondary role, emerges as an embodiment of cultural and communal wisdom in the plot of black women's works.

Representative works in this study of black women who published during the slavery, Reconstruction, and Harlem Renaissance periods from Harriet Jacobs's *Incidents in the Life of a Slave Girl* (1861) to Jessie Redmon Fauset's *Comedy: American Style* (1933) portray the image of the redefined foremother figure. In these early works the foremother is inscribed in speech situations which result in a direct or indirect impact on the life of the mulatta heroine or principal character. That is, despite her minor role as the older black woman, the foremother uses words that invariably influence the principal black female character because her language reflects her view of the world—the view of black cultural knowledge, which conflicts with the view of the prevailing dominant ideology. Elements of this prevailing ideology are often incorporated in the mulatta's world view; however, following a situation that permits the indirect or direct flow of language from the foremother to the mulatta, specific responses from the mulatta occur in the forms of language activity, decisions, and/or actions which can be linked to the foremother's language use. A clear example occurs in Harper's *Minnie's Sacrifice*. After Minnie hears Mrs. Heston's story laced with determination despite racist oppression, Minnie, following the revelation of her mixed heritage, embraces her blackness. Minnie not only embraces her blackness, and her culture but willingly joins forces with her husband to work for the uplift of her people. Whether the impact comes from a specific utterance or a general concept, the close reading offered in this study reveals how the foremother and mulatta heroine are positioned in texts so that the links between the language of the foremother and the decisions and actions of the mulatta heroine or principal character are well-defined. Although critics have noted that subversion of stereotypes, including the mammy, was a major preoccupation of early black writers, this study substantiates the subversion of the mammy stereotype specifically in the foremother-mulatta relationship as a discursive practice in a broad range of early black women's works. This study, in fact, models one of the highest goals of discourse analysis, which is to reveal communicative power structures (Groden and Kreiswirth 1995, 209). These communicative power structures are known to have existed in the hierarchical relationships inherent in the institution of slavery, but have been undemonstrated in the relationship between the secondary older black woman character and the primary younger black woman in the works of early black women writers.

Does the foremother perform the same functions and make the same impact on the life of the principal character in later works of black women writers?

This study will conclude by glancing at representative works of later periods such as Zora Neale Hurston's *Their Eyes Were Watching God* (1937), published during the late Harlem Renaissance period, Ann Petry's *The Street* (1946), published during the period of urban naturalism, and Gloria Naylor's *Mama Day* (1988), a contemporary novel. Modern and contemporary black female works show the foremother making a transition from a figure lacking in prominence but influencing the life of the mulatta heroine to a figure moving toward prominence and controlling major aspects of the life of the principal female character. The foremother's controlling discourse in these modern works leads to psychological development in the mulatta heroine, compelling her to make changes in her personal and family life (though not so much to strive to address the needs of the local community and the society of blacks as a whole). Such an emerging role has been noted by Veta Smith Tucker and K. Sue Jewell, who have observed both permanence and change in the figure of the older black woman in the literature. Tucker sees the mammy figure as corrected, developed, and transformed in contemporary works of black women writers (1994, 2), whereas Jewell observes that images of African American women based on myths and stereotypes continue to resurface only to be challenged, modified, and temporarily eliminated (1993, 183).

HURSTON'S NANNY

Like the foremother Mrs. Harcourt in *Trial and Triumph* and Aunt Sal in *The Chinaberry Tree*, Nanny possesses an intense desire to control and change the circumstances of the principal character, Janie; however, like Annette and Laurentine reflect varying degrees of rejection of the foremother's wisdom, so does Janie.

Nanny, the foremother in *Their Eyes Were Watching God* (1937) by Zora Neale Hurston, helps to define the quadroon heroine, Janie Crawford, through the power of her words when she says, "'Janie youse a 'oman now'" (12). Nanny ushers Janie to the path of protective matrimony with these words because she wishes to protect Janie from acts of violence. Just as Nanny conceived her daughter as a result of institutionalized rape during enslavement, Nanny's daughter conceived

Janie as a result of the vestiges of institutionalized rape following slavery. On the basis of this dual experience, Nanny thus reacts to what she sees as the potential violation of her 16-year old granddaughter when she "bolted upright and peered out of the window and saw Johnny Taylor *lacerating* her Janie with a kiss" (11 emphasis added).

Nanny's views reflect her life experiences further when she describes the black woman in general terms of the actions and inactions of white men and black men respectively. She views the black woman as the "mule of the world"—the one who is ultimately responsible for the welfare of the family and community, but who is forced into hard labor and subservience. Nanny explains to Janie: "'So de white man throw down de load and tell de nigger man tah pick it up. He pick it up because he have to, but he don't tote it. He hand it to his womenfolks. De nigger woman is de mule uh de world so fur as Ah can see'" (14). Nanny maintains faith in the male/female relationship, however, regardless of her own personal experience. Nanny holds the view that marriage means protection for women (14) because she has never experienced the bonds of matrimony, and because she uses the white Mr. and Mrs. Washburn as her models for matrimony. She assures Janie when she marries Logan Killicks, "'You got yo' lawful husband same as Mis' Washburn or anybody else!'" (21) Nanny confirms Janie's right to a proper marriage like white people in general, whereas during her life of enslavement, marriage was not legally recognized. A major problem, however, is that Nanny sees marriage as protection but Logan Killicks, Janie's first husband, sees marriage as an opportunity to engage Janie in "mule" responsibilities when he hints, "'Ah aims tuh run two plows, and dis man Ah'm talkin' 'bout is got uh mule all gentled up so even uh woman kin handle 'im'" (26). Janie avoids this harness type of protection planned for her first marriage, but through this initial major life experience, she reveals the evidence of Nanny's controlling language when she too uses the Washburns later as a standard for assessment. When she sees Joe Starks come along, she compares his gait and posture to that of Mr. Washburn: "He whistled, mopped his face and walked like he knew where he was going. He was a seal-brown color but he acted like Mr. Washburn or somebody like that" (26). Like Nanny, Janie uses the Washburn name in the speech context of asserting a natural right.

Nanny accelerates her controlling language when she explains to Janie that she does not have to contend with the restraints of slavery and encourages her to excel—to elevate her status through marriage.

She uses the power of the word to convince Janie to "'just take a stand on high ground lak Ah dreamed'" (16). These words may well be part of Janie's motive in following Joe Starks, whose ambition will carry her into a higher sphere than her menial work for Logan Killicks. Nanny's use of the language becomes a tool of instruction because Janie learns about the power of language from Nanny. Joanne Gabbin says that Janie learns about the power of language to recreate reality, to reconstruct the past, and to construct the parameters for the future (251). Janie recreates reality later when she creates an audience of one to tell her dying husband, Joe Starks, how he had refused to listen to her during their 20-year marriage. In her recreation of reality, Janie eliminates the probability that Joe Starks will no longer hear her: "'Ah knowed you wasn't goin tuh lissen tuh me. You changes everything but nothin' don't change you—not even death. But Ah ain't goin outa here and Ah ain't gointuh hush'" (82). Janie reconstructs the past when she realizes that what Nanny wanted for her is not what she desired for herself and that Nanny's values were limited by her experience in another era as she tells her best friend:

> "Ah done lived Grandma's way now Ah means tuh live mine. . . . She was borned in slavery time when folks, dat is black folks, didn't sit down anytime dey felt like it. So sittin' on porches lak de white madam looked lak uh mighty fine thing tuh her. Dat's whut she wanted for me—don't keer whut it cost. . . . So Ah got up on de high stool lak she told me, but Pheoby, Ah done nearly languished tuh death up dere" (108-09).

Thus even though Janie has come to reject Nanny's advice and to regret having followed it too long, she still enacts Nanny's deeper influence—empowerment through language. Janie soon assumes agency and constructs the parameters of the future when she chooses Tea Cake as her soul mate (119) despite the community's disapproval.

Janie eventually goes against the wishes of the community, but what she wants does not come to fruition until she has first fulfilled the expressed wishes of the foremother. Janie avoids a random adolescent sexual encounter by accepting Nanny's criticism of her first kiss: "'Ah don't want no trashy nigger, no breath-and-britches, lak Johnny Taylor usin' yo body to wipe his foots on.' Nanny's words made Janie's kiss across the gatepost seem like a manure pile after a rain" (12). Nanny tells Janie why she must marry Logan Killicks: "'Tain't Logan Killicks

Ah wants you to have, baby, it's protection'" (14). Janie obediently marries Logan Killicks and experiences a loveless marriage of protection. She then marries Joe Starks, whose discourse alludes to the status that Nanny had hoped for Janie: "'A pretty doll-baby lak you is made to sit on de front porch and rock and fan yo'self'" (28). Joe Starks promises more status and fun, but she experiences an oppressive relationship on the high stool on the high road. Janie realizes the extent of Nanny's influence in her life when she later concludes that Nanny's vision was clouded with the notion that materialism and marriage are prerequisites for attaining a "higher ground." Janie seeks the depths of human resources rather than the surface of material resources in her search for wholeness. She wants a relationship based on love, which brings with it its own form of protection, a relationship soon found with Tea Cake. Under the controlling language of her grandmother Janie acquires from experience a very clear perspective of what she does not want and most importantly of what she does want in the person of Tea Cake. Janie carves her own reality out of her life experiences—life experiences that were navigated by the language of the foremother, Nanny.

PETRY'S GRANNY

In Ann Petry's *The Street* (1946) Lutie's grandmother, like Janie's grandmother in *Their Eyes Were Watching God* (1937) saw, ironically, that marriage to men existed as protection from men. Trudier Harris points out that Lutie's grandmother wanted Lutie to marry young so that men would not take advantage of her because of her beauty (1982, 88). Again the foremother emerges in the form of the grandmother of the principal character. The fact that she appears only in Lutie's brief memories is exemplary of the depth and range of the foremother figure which emerges through discourse. Lutie paints a substantive portrait of the foremother and acknowledges her connection and influence in her life, even though on a rational level she is skeptical of her grandmother's special powers:

> you couldn't be brought up by someone like Granny without
> absorbing a lot of nonsense that would spring at you out of
> nowhere . . . and when you least expected it. All those tales about
> things that people sensed before they actually happened. Tales that
> had been handed down and down and down until, if you tried to trace

them back, you'd end up God knows where—probably Africa. And
Granny had them all at the tip of her tongue (15-16).

Lutie not only credits the source of her own perception, but she also
traces the origin of the foremother's gift of perception to traditional
African culture. Although Lutie is critical of second-sight and
alternative ways of knowing, she engages in and relies on these mental
activities because they are interwoven into her life experience. Lutie
engages in such powers of perception when she attempts to deal with
her morbid feelings: "She was afraid of something. What was it? She
didn't know. It wasn't just fear of what would happen to Bub. It was
something else. She was smelling out evil as Granny said. An old, old
habit. Old as time itself " (413). Lutie recalls her Grandmother's words
when the white Mr. Crosse harasses her following a singing interview:
"Yes . . . if you were born black and not too ugly, this is what you get"
(321). Lutie can see the cords of wickedness controlled by white men
(Crosse's and Junto's harassment) because of the foremother's warning,
"'Lutie baby, don't you never let no white man put his hands on
you. . . . Don't you never let any of 'em touch you'" (45).

Lutie realizes that her grandmother's words have become a part of
her, much like breathing (46). The foremother's words control an
aspect of her life much as breathing facilitates life. Confirming the
influence of the foremother's words is Lutie's admission that her
distrust and dislike of white men are greater than the white female's
distrust and dislike for her, an attractive black woman (46). It is Mrs.
Chandler's white friends who cast Lutie as the stereotypical wench.
This prejudgment prevails not only because of her black race, but
because of the dominant society's prescription of class and description
of beauty. Christian observes that Petry's female characters are
intended to counteract stereotypical forms. Although Lutie is brown-
skinned, she fits the stereotypical tragic mulatta portrait because she is
cut off from the community, and because she is beautiful but does not
use her beauty for financial gain. Christian says that Lutie has the soul
of Iola Leroy because she counteracts the assumed equation that lower
class, plus attractive black female, equals prostitution.

Adding to Christian's comparison of Lutie Johnson and Iola Leroy
is the evidence that Lutie initially uses the dominant culture as a
standard in her perception of success, despite her grandmother's
warning that she protect herself from those who hold the power. In her
ignorance Lutie omits the race factor and believes that if one desires to

succeed and works hard, then one will succeed. She falls under the influence of competitive individualism when "After a year of listening to their [the Chandlers'] talk, she absorbed some of the same spirit" (Petry *The Street* 43). Likewise, after years of a white education and the influence of a white society, Iola perceives Aunt Linda's dialect features to be amusing and quaint (Harper *Iola Leroy* 175); therefore, she still holds the language of the dominant culture to be correct and the standard by which to measure all other varieties of the language. As Christian points out, however, Lutie and Iola do counteract stereotypical forms. Another way in which Lutie counteracts stereotypical forms is that she works as a maid but does not fit the stereotypical mammy image (1980, 65). Lutie perceives her domestic work as a means to an end, not an end in itself (Harris 1982, 89), unlike those characters who were cast in the role of Mammy in early white female works.

As Granny influences Lutie, it is evident that Lutie influences her eight-year-old son, Bub, when he remembers her lecture about the link between the expectation of white people and his desire to shine shoes in order to earn income (336). Lutie attempts to raise Bub's consciousness so that he can realize the serious and lasting implications of his wish to earn money shining shoes. Ironically, Bub is brave enough to work on the street, but afraid to sleep at home alone. Lutie recalls that she did not fear the darkness like Bub when she was young because Granny was always there accompanied with the familiar sounds of humming and rocking. Granny was in a very positive way a part of the darkness (404).

Granny's words of advice to Lutie, "never let no white man put his hands on you," reverberate throughout the novel as the meaning of the words changes from prevention to pro-action. Lutie expresses repeatedly that she wants to kill the powerful white male, Junto. She initially expresses her desire in the subjunctive mode, "'I would like to kill him'" (422). Such an expressed desire goes beyond the foremother's advice. Lutie's desire, however, evolves even further beyond the semantic level of the foremother's advice when she leaps from the verbally subjunctive mode to the physically active mode and beats black Boots Smith to death because he sanctions white Junto's desire to further manipulate and constrict every aspect of her life. Lutie enacts Granny's words, but takes them to a higher and broader level when on the brink of despair she is "striking at the white world which thrust black people into a walled enclosure from which there was no escape" (430). Although Granny's presence emerges only through Lutie's memory, she still controls areas of Lutie's life because of the power of her words—words that Lutie often criticized but words that shaped her vision, her decision, and her action.

NAYLOR'S *MAMA DAY*

Gloria Naylor's *Mama Day* (1988) presents dual foremother figures in the characters of Mama Day and Abigail, similar to Emma Dunham Kelley's combined foremother persona of Mrs. Randal and Elsie in *Megda* (1891). Abigail and Mama Day help, in the absence of the dead mother, to define the principal character, Ophelia, in this most recent work in this study. The duality of the foremother figure is readily apparent. The narrator says that Mama Day and Abigail are so close that they "ain't gotta look at each other to exchange a smile" (114). Mama Day recognizes their singularity and their duality when she thinks, "'We're like two peas in a pod, but we're two peas still the same'" (153). Ophelia recognizes the dual nature of the foremother and attempts to explain it to George: "'But if Grandma had raised me alone, I would have been ruined for any fit company. It seemed I could do no wrong with her, while with Mama Day I could do no right. I guess, in a funny kind of way, together they were the perfect mother'" (58).

The dual foremother figure of Mama Day and Abigail not only speaks with one voice, but writes with one voice. Their written communication to Ophelia is a single production resulting from a dual effort as they discuss the contents of a letter before Abigail puts the contents into written form. Ophelia says of their letters, "'The same old news from home, but if those letters had ever stopped coming, I don't know what I'd do'" (122).

This dynamic dual foremother figure embodies numerous characteristics associated with the foremother. Mama Day and Abigail use their influence through the mediums of the language and the spirit. They possess and pass on wisdom by relying on memory and the word. Mama Day is timeless because she says that she is not going to die (7). The text reveals the depth of Mama Day's spirituality when the narrator says that she can look at sounds when she visits "the other place" (284). Because Mama Day is in tune with all forms of nature, her perception is such that before she actually knows, she is keenly aware that "there's something waiting for me to know" (118).

The desire for connection and linkage is reciprocal in this relationship between foremother and principal female character just as home is central for the trio. Ophelia says that they could never forgive her for staying away (19) and at the same time she admits, "'God, I wanted to go home—and I meant, home home'" (22). Home symbolizes the twin homes in which she was pampered and protected by Abigail and corrected and instructed by Mama Day. Mama Day cherishes the ties that bind her and Ophelia because she assisted with her birth and participated in the selection of her names—Ophelia, Baby Girl, and Cocoa. It is both a spiritual bond drawn from the generative power of words, and, as Larry Andrews observes, a "union beyond words" that unite Ophelia and Mama Day with each other and with nature (299).

Mama Day's insight goes beyond words indeed, for she reads not only the face in general, but the mouth, throat, lips, neck and shoulder movements (38) to determine meaning that lies below the level of language. Ophelia describes Mama Day as "always having a way of seeing right through people and their motives" (57). Ophelia, too, possesses to a limited degree this power of perception. She can see in George's face that he wanted to hire her (50). She also knows, without seeking an explanation, that Abigail and Mama Day's gift of a quilt is not for exhibition but for everyday use (147). Ophelia is, however, not fully aware of her power, and, as Andrews points out, "she is not fully aware of her foremother tradition, those that came before" (297).

The foremother, Mama Day, is the eldest in Willow Springs; therefore, she embodies the powers of historical knowledge, experience, and wisdom. Her very being demands respect from within the community (51) and outside the community. It is because of her gifted hands that Dr. Smithfield addresses Mama Day as a medical colleague when he visits her patients in Willow Springs (85). She is holistic in her approach to health care in that she places emphasis on believing (mental/emotional), listening (aural), and seeing (visual) (90). Mama Day tells Ophelia that "'folks see what they want to see. . . . And for them to see what's really happening here [the other place], they gotta be ready to believe'" (97). Mama Day is a custodian of spiritual powers and practices as it is represented in the yellow powder that helps Ophelia acquire a job, and the lightening that strikes Ruby's house in order to protect Ophelia. Ophelia is protected so that she can be brought into the full knowledge of her tragic family history. She possesses and cherishes the wealth of knowledge about her family originating with Sapphira Wade, who is the foremother of foremothers of the Day family's African American legacy.

The legacy of the foremother reflects a figure that is influential through language whether she is barely perceptible, secondary, dual, singular, memorable, critical, rigid, indirect, or direct and primary as Naylor's Mama Day. Mama Day not only defines the principal female character but controls her space with her words, beliefs, and actions. She is, in this contemporary work, primary, direct, and powerful—so powerful that not just a Chapter bears her name, as in the case of Jacobs's Aunt Nancy, but a book.

As this study has suggested, the foremother figure, modified in the early works of black women writers but often wrongly presumed to be the stereotypical mammy that appears in the early works of white women writers, serves a greater socio-cultural function than simply a physical foil, as in Aunt Henny's "coal-black kindly face" (33) standing in contrast to Hagar's "pure creamy skin" (35) in *Hagar's Daughter* by Pauline Hopkins. Aunt Henny's and Hagar's features are diminished in light of the large and complex issues that abound in the text. More modern texts show little or no textual emphasis on physical features of the older black women such as Hurston's Nanny, Petry's Granny, and Naylor's Mama Day. Nanny is depicted figuratively through Janie's emotional eyes: "her head and face looked like the standing roots of some old tree that had been torn away by storm" (12). Petry provides no description of Granny's appearance in *The Street*, while it is only George, an outsider to Willow Springs, who reveals that Mama Day has a small frame and is approximately five feet tall (176). Jewell observes that most of the changes that occur in traditional images over time affect the physical rather than the emotional make-up of the older black woman (1993, 183). The physical is more subdued in modern than in early black women's works. Most important, however, is that the spirit of the language in modern black women's works conveys messages that control aspects of the life of the principal character.

This study has emphasized not only the non-physical attributes of the foremother figure but how the range and depth of her persona emerge through her language. For example, the foremother is barely perceptible in Frances Harper's *Minnie's Sacrifice* (1869) and Amelia Johnson's *The Hazeley Family* (1894). Both show how an indirect relationship—Minnie's with grandmother Miriam—and indirect discourse—in the form of harsh criticism of Flora from Aunt Sarah—can influence the life of the mulatta heroine. Yet in Fauset's *Plum Bun*,

Hetty, the foremother, is vividly portrayed in an obvious direct relationship with the mulatta heroine and with an obvious influence which results in the development of a new perspective for this heroine, Angela Murray.

Whether the foremother is barely perceptible or boldly visible, her language reveals that she is the life-force that nurtures her own culture and makes an attempt to repel the influences of the dominant culture. The foremother is a meaningful mainstay in early and modern works of black women writers. Modern black women writers use the same cultural resource of the older and wiser black woman figure as their earlier sisters did. These later writers draw from the same source that influenced early readers. The source of power that makes a difference and attempts to make a difference in individual lives, families, and whole communities is the foremother, not the figure which is so often perceived in the foreground to be working to uplift the race—a presumed leader of the masses, namely the mulatta heroine or principal character in the works of early and later black women writers.

Alice Childress says to writers, "be wary of those who tell you to leave the past alone and confine yourselves to the present moment. Our story has not been told in any moment" (1974, 29). Black women who tell their story rebuild their culture by restoring the communal heritage of sharing, which acts as sustenance for survival. Na'im Akbar calls this sustenance "intuitive collective knowledge" and credits this knowledge for the resilience in black folks ("Reclaiming Ourselves" audio recording). The foremother represents the spiritual visionary who resides in the present, but possesses knowledge of the future with the same level of assurance that she possesses knowledge of the past.

My work, then, constructs a more humanistic vision of the older black woman in black women's fictional works. This humanistic vision, the foremother figure, not only revises the stereotypical mammy but firmly opposes this stereotypical figure, which consistently negates a character with meaningful presence in black women's works. Clearly adhering to an Afrocentric rhetoric, my construction of the foremother figure stands in direct opposition to an aspect of Western culture that has traditionally negated the older black woman in early American literature in general. Bell hooks states that "unless we share ways of rethinking and revisioning with a larger audience, we risk perpetuating the stereotype" (1989, 82). My study not only rethinks and revises, but renames in order to reduce the risk of perpetuating the stereotype. By renaming and illuminating the language of the foremother figure in the context of the mulatta heroine or principal character, this studyfurther expands the breadth of reader responses pertaining to character portrayal in black women's works of fiction.

In addition to this study, we can reduce the risk of perpetuating the mammy stereotype through, for example, a comparative investigation of the works of black women contemporary writers, who look back to the periods of slavery and Reconstruction, and black women who published during these early periods in order to illuminate the intertextuality of character portrayal and language associated with the foremother figure in various speech and situational contexts. In these various contexts the reader will find the foremother in full command of the generative power of the word, because she is clothed in her right mind.

Bibliography

Akbar, Na'im. 1997. Reclaiming Ourselves. Audiotape of a live series of lectures. Tallahassee: Mind Productions and Associates, Inc.

Andrews, Larry. 1993. Black Sisterhood in Naylor's Novels. In *Gloria Naylor: Critical Perspectives Past and Present*, edited by Henry Louis Gates, Jr., and K. A. Appiah. New York: Amistad.

Asante, Molefi K. 1992. Locating a Text: Implications of Afrocentric Theory. In *Language and Literature: the African American Imagination*, edited by Carol Aisha Blackshire-Belay. Westport, CT: Greenwood Press.

———. 1987. *The Afrocentric Idea*. Philadelphia: Temple University Press.

Baym, Nina. 1978. *Woman's Fiction: A Guide to Novels By and About Women in America, 1820-1870*. Ithaca: Cornell University Press.

Birnbaum, Michele A. 1995. 'Alien Hands': Kate Chopin and the Colonization of Race. In *Subjects and Citizens: Nation, Race, and Gender from Oroonoko to Anita Hill*, edited by Michael Moon and Cathy N. Davidson. Durham: Duke University Press.

Boren, Lynda S. 1992. Introduction to *Kate Chopin Reconsidered: Beyond the Bayou*, edited by Lynda S. Boren and Sara deSaussure Davis. Baton Rouge: Louisiana State University Press.

Brookhart, Mary Hughes. 1993. Spiritual Daughters of the Black American South. In *The Female Tradition in Southern Literature*, edited by Carol S. Manning. Urbana: University of Illinois Press. Quoting Paule Marshall. 1983. *Praisesong for the Widow*. New York: Putnam's.

Brooks, Kristina. 1996. Mammies, Bucks, and Wenches: Minstrelsy, Racial Pornography, and Racial Politics in Pauline Hopkins's *Hagar's Daughter*. In *The Unruly Voice: Rediscovering Pauline Elizabeth Hopkins*, edited by John Cullen Gruesser. Chicago: University of Illinois.

Campbell, Jane. 1986. *Mythic Black Fiction: The Transformation of History.* Knoxville: The University of Tennessee Press. Quoting Pauline Hopkins [1899] *Contending Forces: A Romance Illustrative of Negro Life North and South* (Miami: Mnemosyne, 1969), 23.

Carby, Hazel V. 1987. *Reconstructing Womanhood: The Emergence of the Afro-American Woman Novelist.* New York: Oxford University Press.

Childress, Alice. 1974. The Negro Woman in Literature. In *Keeping the Faith: Writings by Contemporary Black American Women.* Edited by Pat Crutchfield Exum. Greenwich, CT: Fawcett Publications, Inc.

Chopin, Kate. [1894] 1969. A No-Account Creole. Vol. 1, *The Complete Works of Kate Chopin,* edited by Per Seyersted. Baton Rouge: Louisiana State University Press.

———. [1894] 1969. Beyond the Bayou. Vol. 1, *The Complete Works of Kate Chopin,* edited by Per Seyersted. Baton Rouge: Louisiana State University Press.

———. [1894] 1969. La Belle Zoraïde. Vol. 1, *The Complete Works of Kate Chopin,* edited by Per Seyersted. Baton Rouge: Louisiana State University Press.

———. [1899] 1993. *The Awakening.* Edited by Nancy A. Walker. Boston: Bedford Books of St. Martin's Press.

Christian, Barbara. 1980. *Black Women Novelists: The Development of a Tradition, 1892-1976.* Westport, CT: Greenwood Press.

———. 1985. *Black Feminist Criticism: Perspectives on Black Women Writers.* New York: Pergamon Press.

——— [1890] 1988. Introduction to *The Hazeley Family,* edited by Henry Louis Gates, Jr. New York: Oxford University Press.

———. 1990. Somebody Forgot to Tell Somebody Something: African American Women's Historical Novels. In *Wild Women in the Whirlwind: Afra-American Culture and the Contemporary Literary Renaissance,* edited by Joanne M. Braxton and Andree Nicola McLaughlin. New Brunswick: Rutgers University Press.

Culler, Jonathan. 1992. Literary Theory. In *Introduction to Scholarship in Modern Languages and Literatures,* edited by Joseph Gibaldi. New York: The Modern Language Association of America.

Cutter, Martha J. 1996. DISMANTLING 'THE MASTER'S HOUSE': Critical Literacy in Harriet Jacobs' *Incidents in the Life of a Slave Girl. Callaloo* 19 no. 1: 209-225.

Davis, Thadious. 1995. Introduction to *Comedy: American Style* by Jessie Redmon Fauset. New York: G.K. Hall & Co.

Donovan, Josephine. 1991. *Uncle Tom's Cabin: Evil, Affliction, and Redemptive Love*. Boston: Twayne Publishers.

Doriani, Beth Maclay. 1991. Black Womanhood in Nineteenth-Century America: Subversion and Self-Construction in Two Women's Autobiographies. *American Quarterly* 43:199-222.

DuCille, Ann. 1993. *The Coupling Convention: Sex, Text, and Tradition in Black Women's Fiction*. New York: Oxford University Press.

Ducksworth, Sara Smith. 1994. Stowe's Construction of African Persons and the Creation of White Identity for a New World Order. In *The Stowe Debate: Rhetorical Strategies in Uncle Tom's Cabin*, edited by Mason I. Lowance, Jr., Ellen E. Westbrook, and R.C. DeProspo. Amherst: University of Massachusetts Press.

Elfenbein, Anna Shannon. 1989. *Women on the Color Line: Evolving Stereotypes and the Writings of George Washington Cable, Grace King, and Kate Chopin*. Charlottesville: University Press of Virginia.

Ernest, John. 1995. *Resistance and Reformation in Nineteenth-Century African-American Literature*. Jackson: University Press of Mississippi.

Ewell, Barbara. 1992. Kate Chopin and the Dream of Female Selfhood. In *Kate Chopin Reconsidered: Beyond the Bayou*, edited by Lynda S. Boren and Sara de Saussure Davis. Baton Rouge: Louisiana State University Press.

Fauset, Jessie Redmon. 1924. *There Is Confusion*. New York: Boni and Liveright.

———. [1928] 1990. *Plum Bun: A Novel Without a Moral*. Introduction. Deborah E. McDowell. Boston: Beacon Press.

———. [1931] 1995. *The Chinaberry Tree: A Novel of American Life*. New York: G.K. Hall & Co.

———. [1933]. 1995. *Comedy: American Style*. New York: G. K. Hall & Co.

Faust, Drew Gilpin. 1996. *Mothers of Invention: Women of the Slaveholding South in the American Civil War*. Chapel Hill: The University of North Carolina Press.

Foster, Frances Smith. 1985. Adding Color and Contour to Early American Self-Portraitures: Autobiographical Writings of Afro-American Women. In *Conjuring: Black Women, Fiction, and Literary Tradition*, edited by Marjorie Pryse and Hortense J. Spillers. Bloomington: Indiana University Press.

———. [1892] 1988. Introduction to *Iola Leroy or Shadows Uplifted* by Frances E. W. Harper, edited by Henry Louis Gates. New York: Oxford University Press.

———. 1993. *Written by Herself: Literary Production by African American Women, 1746-1892*. Bloomington: Indiana University Press.

————. 1994. Introduction to the reprint, *Minnie's Sacrifice, Sowing and Reaping, Trial and Triumph: Three Rediscovered Novels by Frances E. W. Harper*, edited by Frances Smith Foster. Boston: Beacon Press.

————. ed. 1990. *A Brighter Coming Day: A Frances Ellen Watkins Harper Reader*. New York: The Feminist Press.

Gabbin, Joanne V. 1990. A Laying on of Hands: Black Women Writers Exploring the Roots of Their Folk and Cultural Tradition. In *Wild Women in the Whirlwind: Afra-American Culture and the Contemporary Literary Renaissance*, edited by Joanne M. Braxton and Andree Nicola McLaughlin. New Brunswick: Rutgers University Press.

Geist, Christopher D., and Angela M. S. Nelson. 1992. From the Plantation to Bel-Air: A Brief History of Black Stereotypes. In *Popular Culture: An Introductory Text*, edited by Jack Nachbar and Kevin Lause. Bowling Green: Bowling Green University Popular Press.

Graham, Maryemma and Gina M. Rossetti. 1996. Review of the reprint, *Minnie's Sacrifice, Sowing and Reaping, Trial and Triumph: Three Rediscovered Novels* by Frances E. W. Harper, edited by Frances Smith Foster. *African American Review* 30:302-304.

Groden, Michael and Martin Kreiswirth, eds. 1994. *The Johns Hopkins Guide to Literary Theory and Criticism*. Baltimore: The Johns Hopkins University Press.

Gwin, Minrose G. 1985a. *Black and White Women of the Old South: The Peculiar Sisterhood in American Literature*. Knoxville: The University of Tennessee Press,

————. 1985b. Green-eyed Monsters of the Slavocracy: Jealous Mistresses in Two Slave Narratives. In *Conjuring: Black Women, Fiction, and Literary Tradition*, edited by Marjorie Pryse and Hortense J. Spillers. Bloomington: Indiana University Press.

Harper, Frances E. W. [1869] 1994. *Minnie's Sacrifice*. [1876-77] *Sowing and Reaping*. [1888-89] *Trial and Triumph*. Reprinted as *Minnie's Sacrifice, Sowing and Reaping, Trial and Triumph: Three Rediscovered Novels by Frances E. W. Harper*, edited by Frances Smith Foster. Boston: Beacon Press.

————. [1892] 1988. *Iola Leroy or Shadows Uplifted*. Edited by Henry Louis Gates. New York: Oxford University Press.

Harris, Trudier. 1982. *From Mammies to Militants: Domestics in Black American Literature*. Philadelphia: Temple University Press.

Hentz, Caroline Lee. 1854. *The Planter's Northern Bride*. 2 vols. Philadelphia: Parry and McMillan.

Hernton, Calvin C. 1987. *The Sexual Mountain and Black Women Writers: Adventures in Sex, Literature and Real Life.* New York: Doubleday.

hooks, bell. 1989. *Talking Back: Thinking Feminist, Thinking Black.* Boston: South End Press.

Hopkins, Pauline. [1901-02] 1988. *Hagar's Daughter: A Story of Southern Caste Prejudice.* Reprinted in *The Magazine Novels of Pauline Hopkins.* Edited by Henry Louis Gates. New York: Oxford University Press.

———. [1902-03] 1988. *Of One Blood or the Hidden Self.* Reprinted in *The Magazine Novels of Pauline Hopkins.* Edited by Henry Louis Gates. New York: Oxford University Press, 1988.

Hull, Gloria. 1985. 'What Is It I Think She's Doing Anyhow?': A Reading of Toni Cade Bambara's *The Salt Eaters.* In *Conjuring: Black Women, Fiction, and Literary Tradition*, edited by Marjorie Pryse and Hortense J. Spillers. Bloomington: Indiana University Press.

Hurston, Zora Neale. [1937] 1990. *Their Eyes Were Watching God.* Edited by Henry Louis Gates, Jr. New York: Harper and Row, 1990.

Jacobs, Harriet. [1861] 1987. *Incidents in the Life of a Slave Girl Written By Herself.* Edited by Jean Fagan Yellin. Cambridge: Harvard University Press.

Jewell, K. Sue. 1993. *From Mammy to Miss America and Beyond: Cultural Images and the Shaping of U.S. Social Policy.* New York: Routledge.

Johnson, Amelia E. [1890] 1988. *Clarence and Corinne or God's Way.* Edited by Henry Louis Gates, Jr. New York: Oxford University Press.

———. [1894] 1988. *The Hazeley Family.* Edited by Henry Louis Gates, Jr. New York: Oxford University Press.

Kafka, Phillipa. 1993. *The Great White Way: African American Women Writers and American Success Mythologies.* New York: Garland Publishers.

Kelley, Emma Dunham. [1891] 1988. *Megda.* Edited by Henry Louis Gates, Jr. New York: Oxford University Press.

Lerner, Gerda, ed. 1972. *Black Women in White America: A Documentary History.* New York: Vintage Books-Random House.

McDowell, Deborah. 1985. The Neglected Dimension of Jessie Redmon Fauset. In *Conjuring: Black Women, Fiction, and Literary Tradition*, edited by Marjorie Pryse and Hortense Spillers. Bloomington: Indiana University Press.

———. 1987. The Changing Same: Generational Connections and Black Women Novelists. *New Literary History* 18 no. 2: 281-302.

McLendon, Jacquelyn Y. 1995. *The Politics of Color in the Fiction of Jessie Fauset and Nella Larsen.* Charlottesville: University Press of Virginia.

Morrison, Toni. 1992. *Playing in the Dark: Whiteness and the Literary Imagination*. Cambridge: Harvard University Press.

Naylor, Gloria. 1988. *Mama Day*. New York: Vintage Books, 1988.

Pamplin, Claire. 1995. 'Race' and Identity in Pauline Hopkins's Hagar's Daughter. In *Redefining the Political Novel: American Women Writers, 1797-1901*. Edited by Sharon M. Harris. Knoxville: The University of Tennessee Press.

Petry, Ann. 1946. *The Street*. Boston: Houghton Mifflin.

Prenshaw, Peggy Whitman. 1993. Southern Ladies and the Southern Literary Renaissance. In *The Female Tradition in Southern Literature*. Edited by Carol S. Manning. Urbana: University of Illinois Press.

Schultz, Elizabeth. 1977. 'Free in Fact and at Last': The Images of the Black Woman in Black American Literature. In *What Manner of Woman: Essays on English and American Life and Literature*. Edited by Marlene Springer. New York: New York University Press.

Shillingsburg, Miriam J. 1983. The Ascent of Woman, Southern Style: Hentz, King, Chopin. In *Southern Literature in Transition: Heritage and Promise*. Edited by Philip Castille and William Osborne. Memphis: Memphis State University Press.

Shinn, Thelma J. 1985. The Wise Witches: Black Women Mentors in the Fiction of Octavia E. Butler. In *Conjuring: Black Women, Fiction, and Literary Tradition*, edited by Marjorie Pryse and Hortense Spillers. Bloomington: Indiana University Press.

Stowe, Harriet Beecher. [1852] 1966. *Uncle Tom's Cabin*. New York: Signet Classic.

Sylvander, Carolyn Wedin. 1981. *Jessie Redmon Fauset, Black American Writer*. Troy, NY: The Whitston Publishing Company.

Tate, Claudia. 1992. *Domestic Allegories of Political Desire: The Black Heroine's Text at the Turn of the Century*. New York: Oxford University Press.

⸻. 1985. Pauline Hopkins: Our Literary Foremother. *Conjuring: Black Women, Fiction, and Literary Tradition*, edited by Marjorie Pryse and Hortense Spillers. Bloomington: Indiana University Press.

Tompkins, Jane P. 1985. Sentimental Power: *Uncle Tom's Cabin* and the Politics of Literary History. In *The New Feminist Criticism: Essays on Women, Literature and Theory*. Edited by Elaine Showalter. New York: Pantheon Books.

Tillman, Katherine Davis Chapman. [1893] 1991. *Beryl Weston's Ambition: The Story of an Afro-American Girl's Life*. Reprinted in *The Works of*

Katherine Davis Chapman Tillman. Edited by Claudia Tate. New York: Oxford University Press.

Tucker, Veta Smith. 1994. Reconstructing Mammy: Fictive Reinterpretations of Mammy's Role in the Slave Community and Image in American Culture. Ph.D. diss., The University of Michigan.

Viguerie, Mary Patricia Robinson. 1993. My Dear Ol' Mammy: The Enduring Image of the Mammy in Southern Literature. Ph.D. diss., University of Missouri-Columbia.

Wallace, Michele. 1991. *Black Macho and the Myth of the Superwoman.* New York: Verso.

Wallace-Sanders, Kimberly. 1995. A Peculiar Motherhood: The Black Mammy Figure in American Literature and Popular Iconography, 1824-1965. Ph.D. diss., Boston University.

Walker, Alice. 1983a. If the Present Looks Like the Past, What Does the Future Look Like? In *In Search of Our Mothers' Gardens: Womanist Prose*, edited by Alice Walker. New York: Harcourt Brace Jovanovich, 1983.

————. 1983b. In Search of Our Mothers' Gardens. In *In Search of Our Mothers' Gardens: Womanist Prose*, edited by Alice Walker. New York: Harcourt Brace Jovanovich.

Yarborough, Richard. 1986. Strategies of Black Characterization in *Uncle Tom's Cabin* and the Early Afro-American Novel. In *New Essays on Uncle Tom's Cabin*, edited by Eric J. Sundquist. Cambridge: Cambridge University Press.

Yellin, Jean Fagan. 1981. Written by Herself: Harriet Jacobs' Slave Narrative. *American Literature* 53 no. 3:479-486.

Yellin, Jean Fagan. 1985. Text and Contexts of Harriet Jacobs' *Incidents in the Life of a Slave Girl Written by Herself.* In *The Slave's Narrative*, edited by Charles T. Davis and Henry Louis Gates, Jr. New York: Oxford University Press.

Young, Elizabeth. 1995. Warring Fictions: Iola Leroy and the Color of Gender. In *Subjects and Citizens: Nation, Race, and Gender from Oroonoko to Anita Hill*, edited by Michael Moon and Cathy N. Davidson. Durham: Duke University Press. Quoting Frances E. W. Harper [1892] 1988. *Iola Leroy or Shadows Uplifted.* Edited by Henry Louis Gates. New York: Oxford University Press.

Index